Table of Contents

1. About the Author II

2. Tips for Studying III

3. Tips for the Examination IV

4. Study Time Tracker V

5. Practice Exam I 1

6. Practice Exam I Solutions 15

7. Practice Exam II 34

8. Practice Exam II Solutions 47

1. About the Author

 Ethan McCutcheon is a civil engineer with a passion for knowledge and learning. Coming from the small town of Cleveland, Tennessee, he wanted to pursue his passion for learning by attending the University of Tennessee in Knoxville.

Ethan graduated from UTK in 2021 with a Bachelor's in civil engineering and focuses in geotechnical and structural engineering.

He passed the Fundamentals of Engineering (FE) exam in early 2021 prior to graduating. With a degree in civil engineering and an E.I.T. certification, he started a career that would allow him to fully utilize his knowledge and newly acquired skills.

Ethan then passed the Principles and Practices of Engineering (PE) exam three years before his four-year experience milestone to advance his career at an earlier age.

When free time is available, Ethan likes to develop his skills in photography, guitar, fitness, and blog writing.

2. Tips for Studying

Establishing both an effective study method and regimen are crucial to achieving success in the Civil PE examination. The following are quick and simple tips that can help you utilize your study time in the most effective ways.

1. Set up a study schedule that will allow you to achieve, or get close to, 300 hours of completed study time before sitting for the exam (see page V for an included time log). 300 hours is not required, however, it will drastically increase your chances of passing.

2. Become overly familiar with the NCEES provided manual and standards. Knowing the location of each chapter in the manual along with its respective concepts will aide you in saving much needed time.

3. Accustom yourself to the *ctrl-f* search function and learn how to utilize it without wasting time. The computers provided at the testing facility will be poor in processing power, thus making each word search take a significant amount of time. Learn how to pick out key words that can be easily searched within the PDFs provided.

4. Customize problems that you experience in practice booklets by exchanging the given values, variables, or auxiliary information. Problems provided on the exam have the potential to ask for any variable imaginable, thus making it important to know how to solve for each.

5. Set time aside to complete entire practice exams under time constraint. This will accustom you to the immense time-induced pressure you will experience during the exam. Be keen on solving most problems under six minutes and know when to skip and return to certain problems.

6. Use your NCEES approved calculator during all study time.

7. Keep a list of all concepts/categories that need more practice.

3. Tips for Examination

Sitting for the actual examination is a daunting task and nerve-racking experience to say the least. The following are certain precautions and actions that can be taken to ease the experience and give you the highest chance of success.

1. Arrive at the testing facility a minimum of 30 minutes early.

2. Review the rules and time layout of the exam prior to arriving. You can find documents on the official NCEES website that detail how long the exam will be, optional break length, and other important information in regards to the exam.

3. Examinees are permitted to store both food and drink in a personal locker that is provided on site. It is highly suggested to bring calorie dense foods that are also effective in boosting brain functionality such as blueberries, broccoli, nuts, etcetera.

4. Utilize the built in "flag" function on questions that are more lengthy or more difficult to solve and come back to them at a later time. This allows you to fully complete the first half of the exam and use your leftover time to complete the more difficult questions.

5. Stick to your preprepared testing strategy and avoid becoming dissociated during the test. Remain calm and collected as scrambling for answers will ultimately lead to failure.

4. Study Time Tracker

Below is a useful table that can be filled out in order to track your active study time in hopes of accumulating a significant amount in the end.

Date	Time	Date	Time	Date	Time	Date	Time	Date	Time	Date	Time

5. Practice Exam I

1.   A temporary handrail has been installed to meet the safety requirements of an elevated working platform. The rail is subject to a maximum horizontal point load of 200lb at its highest point and is anchored to concrete with steel bolts. Find the minimum strength of the steel bolts if a factor of safety of 1.5 is implemented.

    A. 2.7 ton
    B. 1.8 ton
    C. 1.1 ton
    D. 0.9 ton

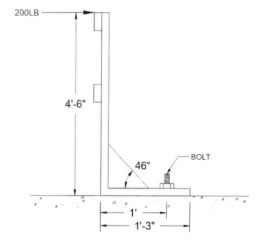

2.   Formwork for a 100ft long concrete wall is to be constructed.

Construction crew #1 consists of two (2) operators, one (1) safety personnel, and three (3) laborers with a production rate of 40ft^2 per hour.

Construction crew #2 consists of one (1) operator, one (1) safety personnel, and three (3) laborers with a production rate of 35ft^2 per hour.

What is the difference in total job price and duration between each crew?

    A. $120 and 1.2 hours
    B. $135.50 and 1.4 hours
    C. $140 and 1 hour
    D. $125.50 and 2.3 hours

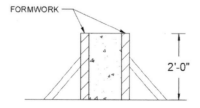

POSITION	RATE PER HOUR
OPERATOR	$35
SAFETY	$40
LABORER	$25

3. The following figure displays a project activity network. Determine the free float for activity C and the total float for activity E.

A. FF=3, TF=1
B. FF=0, TF=1
C. FF=0, TF=0
D. FF=1, TF=1

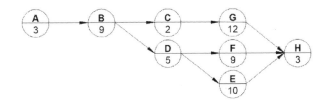

4. In-situ soil is to be hauled out of the following construction site to match the needed elevation. What is most nearly the total loose volume that must be hauled off site if the soil has a swell factor of 12%?

A. 2,500 CY
B. 2,700 CY
C. 3,100 CY
D. 3,500 CY

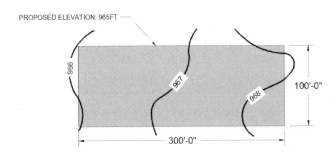

5. A 525ft long drainage canal is to be constructed according to the cross-section below. Assuming a total waste of 5%, what is the total concrete needed?

A. 268 CY
B. 147 CY
C. 151 CY
D. 155 CY

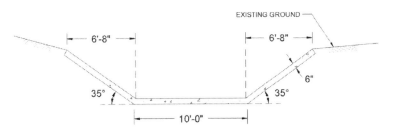

6. Concrete is to be poured during the month of January at a construction site located in northern Wyoming. What type of concrete is least desirable for this pour if sulfate resistance has no importance?

A. Type I
B. Type II
C. Type III
D. Type IV

7. A circular pipe experiences water flow at a consistent depth of 5 inches. With a Manning's roughness coefficient of 0.012 and slope of 1%, find the total flow rate.

A. 612 gpm
B. 742 gpm
C. 560 gpm
D. 628 gpm

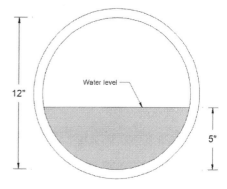

8. Water is to be redirected from an open reservoir through a 6-inch pipe. Given a Hazen-Williams coefficient of 100 and a water flow rate of 100gpm, find the pressure experienced by the pipe at point B if the pipe is flowing full. Account for friction loss in the pipe.

A. 86 psi
B. 90 psi
C. 95 psi
D. 98 psi

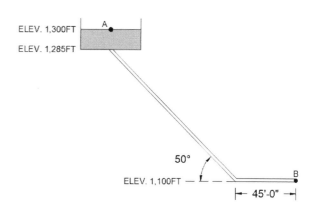

9. What is most nearly the correct order of medians to treat wastewater?

A. Screens→primary clarifier→secondary clarifier→aeration tanks→chlorination and UV disinfection
B. Primary clarifier→secondary clarifier→screens→chlorination and UV disinfection→aeration tanks
C. Screens→aeration tanks→primary clarifier→secondary clarifier→chlorination and UV disinfection
D. Screens→primary clarifier→aeration tanks→secondary clarifier→chlorination and UV disinfection

10. Measurements have been taken from a pitot tube and static pressure tube. Find the velocity of flow.

A. 3 ft/s
B. 7 ft/s
C. 5 ft/s
D. 10 ft/s

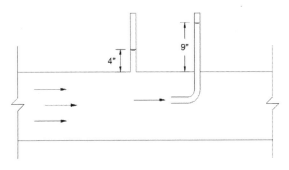

11. A sharp crested weir discharges approximately 200,000gpm. What is the ideal weir length?

A. 20 ft
B. 30 ft
C. 35 ft
D. 45 ft

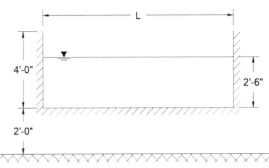

12. Water is flowing full through a parallel set of pipes. Find the velocity of flow through pipe AEFD if all pipes have a diameter of 4".

A. 0.5 ft/s
B. 1.1 ft/s
C. 0.7 ft/s
D. 0.9 ft/s

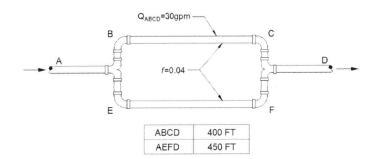

| ABCD | 400 FT |
| AEFD | 450 FT |

13.   A 13ft wide by 10ft long by 5ft tall object with a unit weight of 50lb/ft^3 is placed into water. How deep must the object be in order to reach full buoyancy?

    A. 1 ft
    B. 5 ft
    C. 4 ft
    D. 3 ft

14.   Two nearby watersheds experience a 30-yr rainfall event with an intensity of 2in/hr. A single culvert is responsible for drainage of both watersheds. What is the peak discharge through the culvert?

    A. 9.6 ft^3/s
    B. 10 ft^3/s
    C. 10.3 ft^3/s
    D. 11 ft^3/s

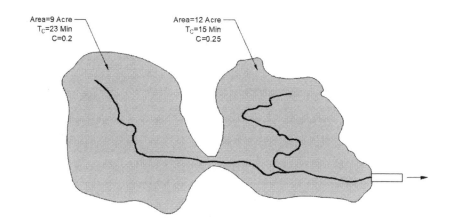

15. A construction site must be dewatered to a depth of 10ft below grade. If an underground aquifer is encountered at a regenerating depth of 5ft below grade, what is the rate of flow that must be drawn from a 1ft diameter well at the center of the site? The aquifer is underlain with an impervious clay layer at a depth of 30ft and water level at the point of the well is successfully lowered to 25ft below grade.

A. 0.03 ft³/s
B. 0.05 ft³/s
C. 0.06 ft³/s
D. 0.08 ft³/s

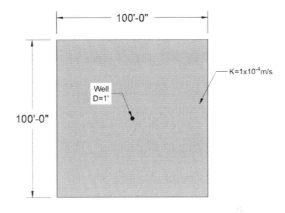

16. Intake flow rate for a primary clarifier is 5,000gpm at a diameter of 40ft. How tall must the clarifier be in order to achieve a 30-minute retention time.

A. 16 ft
B. 20 ft
C. 13 ft
D. 15 ft

17. Who can authorize states to issue stormwater permits under the National Pollutant Discharge Elimination System (NPDES)?

A. Federal Government
B. Environmental Agencies
C. Local and state government
D. Certified OSHA representatives

18.   Headway between cars has been determined to be an average of 7 seconds. If the design highway speed is 55mph, what is most nearly the number of cars per mile?

   A. 3
   B. 5
   C. 8
   D. 10

19.   A car slams its brakes to avoid a pedestrian but collides with a concrete structure in the sand adjacent to the road (Point C). If skid marks are visible on the asphalt for 120ft and the car slides on the sand for 90ft before collision, find the cars original speed before braking (Point A). Speed at collision was determined to be 20mph.

   A. 63 mph
   B. 65 mph
   C. 67 mph
   D. 70 mph

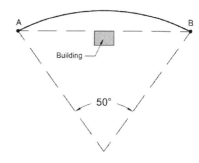

20.   A building is proposed near a curved roadway. If point B must be visible from point A, find the closest distance the building can be located from the center of a 20ft wide road. Degree of curvature if 6.5.

   A. 90 ft
   B. 60 ft
   C. 75 ft
   D. 83 ft

21. Radius for a horizontal curve is 600'. Find the station for PT.

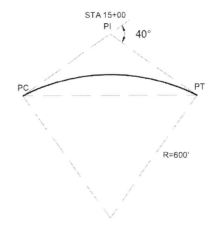

A. 16+50
B. 16+67
C. 17+00
D. 17+55

22. A bridge is to be constructed over a busy road. In order to avoid obstructing visual line of sight with oncoming traffic, the bridge must be a minimum of 20ft above the roadway. What is the minimum elevation required for the lowest point of the bridge?

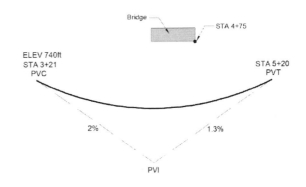

A. 759 ft
B. 752 ft
C. 749 ft
D. 746 ft

23. Determine the station for the point with maximum elevation.

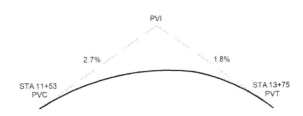

A. 12+86
B. 12+56
C. 12+32
D. 12+12

8

24. A soil was tested for both grain size distribution and plasticity. What is the USCS designation for the soil?

    A. SW
    B. GW
    C. GM
    D. GC

Seive No.	% Passing
No. 4	46
No. 40	20
No. 200	34

Liquid Limit	25
Plastic Limit	13

25. A standard penetration test is performed on a sandy soil. The measured N-values are 32, 35 and 30. If the efficiency of the hammer is measured to be approximately 85%, find the relative density of the soil if adjusting for 60% efficiency.

    A. Very loose
    B. Medium dense
    C. Dense
    D. Very dense

26. A 4ft core is performed on rock substrata. What is the rock quality designation?

    A. Very poor
    B. Poor
    C. Fair
    D. Excellent

27. A saturated soil is tested for relevant properties. What would be the soil unit weight if the soil were located in a highly dry and hot environment such as a desert?

    A. $116 \frac{lb}{ft^3}$
    B. $120 \frac{lb}{ft^3}$
    C. $122 \frac{lb}{ft^3}$
    D. $125 \frac{lb}{ft^3}$

Before Oven Dry	53g
After Oven Dry	46g

Specific Gravity	2.6

28.   What is the factor of safety of slope failure for the given slope?

A. 1.2
B. 1.3
C. 1.5
D. 1.8

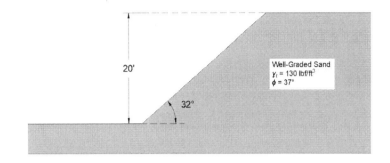

29.   What is the factor of safety against overturn about point A?

A. 1.5
B. 1.9
C. 2
D. 2.2

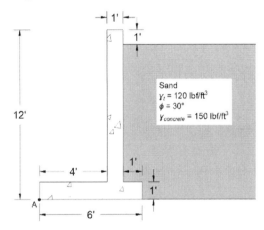

30.   An earthquake is predicted to occur near a local town. Which soil type is most likely to cause the most damage?

A. MH
B. CL
C. GW
D. SW

31. Two footings are located on opposite sides of a building. Which footing is expected to reach ultimate settlement at a quicker rate (left=A, right=B)?

A. Not enough information
B. Footer A
C. Footer B
D. Both experience settlement at the same rate

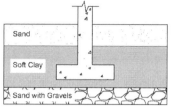 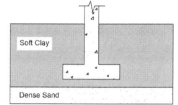

32. Which soil properties can be reliably determined through disturbed sampling?
   I.   Gradation
   II.   Bearing capacity
   III. Classification
   IV.   Compressibility

A. I and III
B. II only
C. III and IV
D. I,II and IV

33. Based on the soil profile below, what is the expected effective stress experienced at point A?

A. $1,674 \frac{lb}{ft^2}$

B. $1,738 \frac{lb}{ft^2}$

C. $1,754 \frac{lb}{ft^2}$

D. $1,802 \frac{lb}{ft^2}$

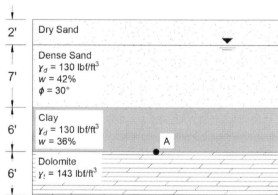

34. Find the allowable bearing capacity for a continuous footing if utilizing a factor of safety of 2 and accounting for depth.

A. $52\dfrac{k}{ft^2}$

B. $55\dfrac{k}{ft^2}$

C. $58\dfrac{k}{ft^2}$

D. $64\dfrac{k}{ft^2}$

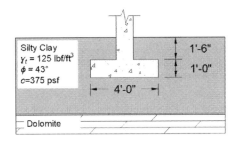

35. A square HSS column is load bearing in a residential basement. Which characteristic of the steel column is most important with regards to critical buckling stress?

A. Column height
B. Unbraced column length
C. Slenderness ratio
D. Cross sectional area

36. A steel cantilever beam is loaded as shown. Find the total deflection to be anticipated.

A. 9 in
B. 7 in
C. 6 in
D. 4 in

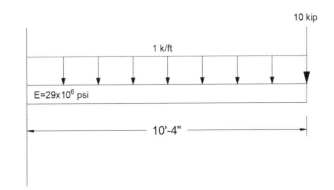
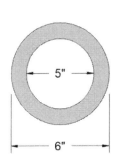

37. A support beam is shown with loading conditions. At which point is the maximum moment encountered?

A. Point A
B. Point B
C. Point C
D. Point D

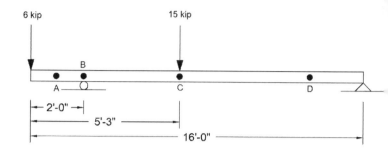

38. A concrete beam undergoes shear failure in the form of a crack. What is most likely the angle of the crack in relation to the horizontal axis. Internal friction angle of the concrete is 31°.

A. 61°
B. 57°
C. 43°
D. 31°

39. A concrete beam has a cross section as follows. What is the nominal moment strength?

A. 127 k-ft
B. 135 k-ft
C. 139 k-ft
D. 143 k-ft

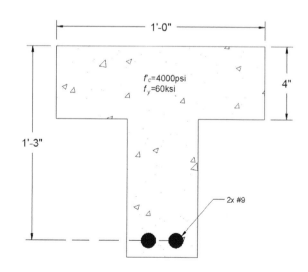

40.   Poisson's Ratio can be best described as the:

   A. Strength of a material
   B. Plastic limit of a material
   C. Ratio of axial strain to lateral strain
   D. Ratio of lateral strain to axial strain

6. Practice Exam I Solutions

No.	Answer	No.	Answer
1	D	21	C
2	B	22	A
3	C	23	A
4	A	24	D
5	A	25	C
6	D	26	C
7	D	27	A
8	A	28	A
9	D	29	B
10	C	30	D
11	B	31	B
12	C	32	A
13	C	33	D
14	A	34	C
15	D	35	C
16	A	36	A
17	B	37	C
18	D	38	A
19	B	39	B
20	D	40	D

1. After quick evaluation, it can be determined that bolt strength will be directly variable based on the amount of moment experienced at the right-most tipping point. Thus meaning that moment should be solved about the rail's tipping point.

Tip: When questions give you a factor of safety, it can often times be crucial to write this value down before solving the problem as to not forget to incorporate it in the end.

Note: The symbol $\therefore$ is utilized as a method to convey "therefore".

$\rightarrow$ Set up moment equation (taking counterclockwise as positive and using decimal feet):

$$\Sigma M_{tip}=0=-200lb(4.5ft)+R_{bolt}(0.25ft)$$

$$\therefore R_{bolt}=3,600lb$$

$\rightarrow$ Apply FOS and convert to ton:

$$Factor\ of\ Safety=1.5=\frac{M_{ult}}{M_{all}}=\frac{M_{ult}}{3,600lb}\ \therefore M_{ult}=5,400lb$$

$$M_{ult}=5,400lbx\frac{1\ ton}{2000lb}=2.7ton\quad \underline{\textbf{Answer:D}}$$

---

2. Wordy problems such as this are best taken one step at a time. Notice that the question is asking for a comparison in total job price and duration meaning that we must first solve for total area of formwork along with the price per hour for each crew.

$\rightarrow$ Find A_{wall}:

$$A_{wall}=2ftx100ftx2walls=400ft^2$$

$\rightarrow$ Find hourly crew rates:

$$Crew\ 1=(2)(\$35)+(1)(\$40)+(3)(\$25)=\$185\ per\ hour$$

$$Crew\ 2=(1)(\$35)+(1)(\$40)+(3)(\$25)=\$150\ per\ hour$$

$\rightarrow$ Find total build time for each crew:

$$Crew\ 1=400ft^2\div40\frac{ft^2}{hr}=10hr$$

$$Crew\ 2=400ft^2\div35\frac{ft^2}{hr}=11.4hr\ \therefore \Delta time=1.4hr$$

$\rightarrow$ Compare total costs:

$$Crew\ 1=10hr\ x\$185\ per\ hour=\$1,850$$

$$Crew\ 2=11.4hr\ x\$150\ per\ hour=\$1,710\ \therefore \Delta cost=\$140\quad \underline{\textbf{Answer: B}}$$

3.   In order to find total and free float, an activity diagram must be created.

→ Create activity diagram:

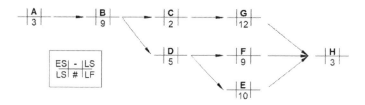

→ Fill out activity diagram with start and finish durations (always begin with 0, not 1):

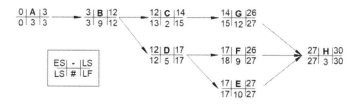

→ Find free float for activity C and total float for E (pg.70, CRH):

Note: CRH refers to the Civil Reference Handbook which is a PDF provided during the test and can be found on the official NCEES website as a downloadable file.

$$FF_C = ES_{Successor} - LS_{predecessor} = ES_G - LS_C = 14 - 14 = \underline{\mathbf{0}}$$

$$TF_E = LS_E - LF_E = 27 - 27 = 0 \quad \underline{\textit{\textbf{Answer: C}}}$$

---

4.   Since three contours are provided, it is most logical to utilize the *prismoidal formula* for volume estimation from three cross sections (pg.49, CRH). Other logical methods could also work for a rough estimation.

→ Find area of cross sections located at each contour:

A	B	C
966ft	967ft	968ft
965ft	965ft	965ft
⊢— 100' —⊣	⊢— 100' —⊣	⊢— 100' —⊣

$$A_A = 100ft(966ft - 965ft) = 100ft^2$$

$$A_B = 100ft(967ft - 965ft) = 200ft^2$$

$$A_C = 100ft(968ft - 965ft) = 300ft^2$$

→ Utilize prismoidal formula:

$$V_{Bank} = L\left(\frac{A_1 + 4A_m + A_2}{6}\right) = (300ft)\left(\frac{100ft^2 + (4)200ft^2 + 300ft^2}{6}\right) = 60,000ft^3$$

→ Apply swell factor (pg.47, CRH) and convert to cubic yards:

Tip: The conversion constant between cubic feet and cubic yards is important to have stored in memory in order to solve problems at a faster pace (1CY=27ft³).

$$V_L=(1+\tfrac{S_w}{100})V_B \therefore V_L=(1+\tfrac{12\%}{100})(60,000ft^3)=67,200ft^3$$

$$67,200ft^3 x\frac{1CY}{27ft^3}=2,488.9CY \therefore 2,500CY \quad \underline{\textbf{\textit{Answer: A}}}$$

---

5.   In order to find total concrete needed, the total surface area should be found first. This can then be multiplied with the concrete thickness to acquire a volumetric quantity.

Tip: Similar to factor of safety, provided waste factors are best written down previous to solving the problem as to not forget incorporation in the end.

→ Solve for length of side walls (using decimal feet):

$$Cos(35°)=\frac{6.667ft}{L} \therefore L=8.139ft$$

$$\therefore L_{Tot}=(2\ walls)(8.139ft)+10ft=26.278ft$$

$$\therefore V_{Tot}=(26.278ft)(Length)(Depth)=(26.278ft)(525ft)(0.5ft)=6987.925ft^3$$

Tip: It is typically best practice to keep values accurate to three decimal places as it can drastically change your answer in select cases unless not needed.

→ Incorporate waste factor and convert to cubic yards:

$$V_{Tot}=(6987.925ft^3)(1+\tfrac{5\%}{100})=7,242.821ft^3$$

$$7,242.821ft^3 x\frac{1CY}{27ft^3}=268CY \quad \underline{\textbf{\textit{Answer: A}}}$$

---

6.   Context clues are a large factor in word-dependent problems. It can be assumed that the pour site will have severe temperature conditions due to the provided location and time of year.

→ Determine least desirable concrete type:

   Type I: General purpose

   Type II: Moderate sulfate resistance

   Type III: High early strength

   Type IV: Low heat of hydration   **Answer: D**

Type V: High sulfate resistance

---

7.   The key word "Manning" can be picked out from this problem to easily find the necessary equation in the reference handbook (pg.345, CRH).

→ Set up Manning's equation with given information:

$$Q=(\frac{1.486}{n})(A)(R)^{2/3}(S)^{1/2}=(\frac{1.486}{0.012})(A)(R)^{2/3}(0.01)^{1/2}$$

→ Find flow area and hydraulic radius with Circular Segment equation (pg.8, CRH):

Note: *Finding flow area and wetting perimeter for flow in a circular pipe requires using radii as opposed to degrees. Make sure to set the calculator to the proper units before and after compositions.*

$$\theta =2(arccos((r-d)/2))=2(arccos((0.5ft-0.417ft)/0.5ft))=2.808rad$$

$$A_{Flow}=(r^2(\theta-sin\,\theta))/2=((0.5ft)^2(2.808rad-sin(2.808rad))/2=0.31ft^2$$

$$Wetted\ perimeter\ (s) \rightarrow \theta=s/r \therefore 2.808rad=s/0.5ft \therefore s=1.404ft$$

$$Hydraulic\ radius\ (R)= \frac{A_{Flow}}{Wetted\ Perimeter}=\frac{0.31ft^2}{1.404ft}=0.221ft$$

→ Solve for Q:

$$Q=(\frac{1.486}{0.012})(0.31ft^2)(0.221ft)^{2/3}(0.01)^{1/2}=1.4\frac{ft^3}{s}\rightarrow 1.4\frac{ft^3}{s}x\frac{1\,gal}{0.1337ft^2}\,x\frac{60\,sec}{1\,min}=\textbf{628gpm}$$

Answer: D

---

8.   The key word "Hazen-Williams" is an easy indicator as to which equation will be essential in the problem. Along with calculated head loss from friction, a conservation of energy equation can be used to find pressure at point B.

→ Use Hazen-Williams for head loss due to friction (pg.328, CHR):

$$h_f=\frac{4.73L}{C^{1.852}D^{4.87}}Q^{1.852}$$

$$Convert\ flow\ rate\ to\ ft^3/s\rightarrow 100\frac{g}{m}x\frac{0.1337ft^3}{1g}x\frac{1m}{60s}=0.223ft^3/s$$

$$Find\ L\rightarrow sin(50°)=\frac{1285ft-1100ft}{L} \therefore L=241.5ft+45ft=286.5ft$$

$$\therefore h_f=\frac{4.73(286.5ft)}{(100)^{1.852}(0.5ft)^{4.87}}(0.223ft^3/s)^{1.852}=0.486ft$$

→ Set up conservation of energy equation:

$$Z_A + \frac{V_A^2}{2g} + \frac{P_A}{\gamma_w} = Z_B + \frac{V_B^2}{2g} + \frac{P_B}{\gamma_w} + h_f$$

Note: V_A and P_A can be assumed as zero due to open air exposure and negligible drain speed from reservoir.

Find $V_B \rightarrow Q_B = V_B A_B$ *(Continuity Equation; pg.306, CRH)*

$0.223 ft^3/s = V_B(\pi(0.25ft)^2) \rightarrow V_B = 1.136 ft/s$

$\therefore (1,300ft) + (0) + (0) = (1,100ft) + \left(\frac{(1.136 ft/s)^2}{2\left(\frac{32.2ft}{s^2}\right)}\right) + \left(\frac{P_B}{62.4\frac{lb}{ft^3}}\right) + 0.486ft$

$\therefore P_B = 12,448.423\frac{lb}{ft^2} x \frac{1ft^2}{144in^2} = \mathbf{86.4psi}$ **_Answer: A_**

---

9.   The correct order for wastewater treatment is as follows:

Screens→primary clarifier→aeration tanks→secondary clarifier→chlorination and UV disinfection

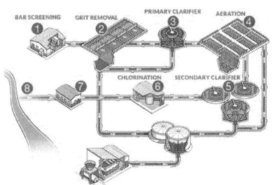

Answer: D

---

10.   Utilize the *Pitot Tube* section (pg.317, CRH) to better visualize pressure head and velocity head.

→ Equate water heights with pressure and velocity head:

$4'' \rightarrow 0.333ft = \frac{P}{\gamma_w}$

$9'' \rightarrow 0.75ft = \frac{P}{\gamma_w} + \frac{V^2}{2g} \therefore 0.75ft = 0.333ft + \frac{V^2}{2\left(\frac{32.2ft}{s^2}\right)} \therefore V = \mathbf{5.182ft/s}$ **_Answer: C_**

11. Utilize sharp-crested weir formula (pg.319, CRH).

→ Use discharge equation:

$$Q=CLH^{3/2}$$

$$C=3.27+0.4(\frac{2.5ft}{2ft})=3.77$$

$$Convert\ flow\ rate \rightarrow 200,000\frac{g}{m}x\frac{1m}{60s}x\frac{0.1337ft^3}{1g}=445.667\frac{ft^3}{s}$$

$$\therefore 445.667\frac{ft^3}{s}=(3.77)(L)(2.5ft)^{3/2}\ \therefore L=29.906ft\quad \underline{\textit{Answer: B}}$$

---

12. In this problem, it is essential to recognize that head loss due to friction is the same for pipes in a parallel series. With this observation, it can be noted that the *Darcy-Weisbach* equation should be used to find head loss (pg.313, CRH).

→ Find velocity for pipe ABCD:

$$Q_{ABCD}=30\frac{g}{m}x\frac{1m}{60s}x\frac{0.1337ft^3}{1g}=0.067\frac{ft^3}{s}$$

$$Q_{ABCD}=V_{ABCD}(A_{ABCD}) \rightarrow 0.067\frac{ft^3}{s}=V_{ABCD}(\pi(\frac{0.333ft}{2})^2)\ \therefore V_{ABCD}=0.769ft/s$$

→ Find head loss for pipe ABCD:

$$(h_f)_{ABCD}=f(\frac{L}{D})(\frac{V^2}{2g})=(0.04)(\frac{400ft}{0.333ft})(\frac{(\frac{0.769ft}{s})^2}{2(\frac{32.2ft}{s^2})})\ \therefore (h_f)_{ABCD}=0.441ft$$

→ Equate head loss of pipe ABCD with pipe AEFD:

$$(h_f)_{ABCD}=(h_f)_{AEFD} \rightarrow 0.441ft=(0.04)(\frac{450ft}{0.333ft})(\frac{(V_{AEFD})^2}{2(\frac{32.2ft}{s^2})})\ \therefore V_{AEFD}=0.725ft/s\ \underline{\textit{Answer: C}}$$

---

13. Submerged volume of the specified object will yield a buoyant force. When the object reaches "full buoyancy", the weight of water displaced will equal the object's total weight.

→ Find total weight of object and equate to volume of water displaced:

$$V_{Object}=13ftx10ftx5ft=650ft^3$$

$$W_{Object}=650ft^3x50\frac{lb}{ft^3}=32,500lb$$

$$32,500lb=(13ftx10ftxDepth\ Submerged)(62.4\frac{lb}{ft^3})\ \therefore \textbf{Depth=4ft}\quad \underline{\textit{Answer: C}}$$

14. Any problem that has relevance to rainfall intensity and watershed runoff will most likely utilize the *Rational Formula Method* (pg.376, CRH).

→ Set up peak discharge formula:

$$Q=CIA \rightarrow Q=C(2\tfrac{in}{hr})(9acre+12acre)$$

→ Find weighted runoff coefficient for both drainage areas (pg.377, CRH):

$$C_w=\frac{9acre(0.2)+12acre(0.25)}{9acre+12acre}=0.229$$

→ Finish peak discharge formula:

$$Q=(0.229)(2\tfrac{in}{hr})(9acre+12acre)=9.6\tfrac{ft^3}{s} \quad \textbf{\textit{Answer: A}}$$

---

15. Dewatering formulas can be found in *Section 2.3.2* (pg.64, CRH).

→ Set up formula for central pump flow rate. Use second formula as *f* is not given:

$$Q_{Pump}=\frac{\pi K(H^2-h^2)}{\ln(\frac{R_o}{r_w})}$$

→ Find input variables:

$$K=(1x10^{-4}\tfrac{m}{s})x\frac{3.281ft}{1m}=3.28x10^{-4}ft/s$$

$$R_o=\sqrt{50ft^2+50ft^2}=70.7ft$$

$$r_w=1ft\div2=0.5ft$$

$$H=30ft-10ft=20ft$$

$$h=30ft-25ft=5ft$$

→ Solve pump rate formula:

$$Q_{Pump}=\frac{\pi(\frac{3.28x10^{-4}ft}{s})(20ft^2-5ft^2)}{\ln(\frac{70.7ft}{0.5ft})}$$

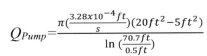

$$Q_{Pump}=0.08\tfrac{ft^3}{s}$$

Answer: D

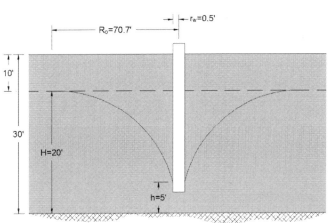

16. Retention time for clarifiers can be found as a direct function of influent flow rate and basin volume.

→ Set up equation:

$$T_{Retention} = V_{Basin} \div Q_{Influent}$$

Convert time to seconds → $T = 30min \times \frac{60s}{1m} = 1,800s$

Convert influent flow rate to ft^3/s → $Q = 5,000\frac{g}{m} \times \frac{0.1337 ft^3}{1g} \times \frac{1m}{60s} = 11.142 ft^3/s$

→ Use original equation to solve for basin height:

$$1,800s = [(\pi(\tfrac{40ft}{2})^2)(H)] \div (11.142 ft^3/s) \therefore H = 16ft \quad \underline{\textit{Answer: A}}$$

---

17. Problems can often times be solved utilizing deductive reasoning, such as the case with this question. It can be reasonably assumed that the only agencies that have proper authority to issue stormwater permits are those related to environmental.

Answer: B

---

18. Headway between vehicles can be defined as the amount of time that passes from the front of one car to the front of the subsequent car. Using this knowledge, the distance between cars can be equated from the assumed speed which can then be used to find the number of cars per mile.

→ Find the distance traveled in 7 seconds:

$$V = 55\frac{mile}{hr} \times \frac{1hr}{60min} \times \frac{1min}{60sec} = 0.015\frac{mile}{sec}$$

$$(D)_{7sec} = 0.015\frac{mile}{sec} \times 7sec = 0.105mile$$

$$\therefore Cars\ per\ mile = 1mile \div 0.105\frac{mile}{car} = \textbf{9.5cars/mile} \quad \underline{\textit{Answer: D}}$$

---

19. Accident analysis problems are made easier if broken down into multiple parts utilizing formulas in *Section 5.1.4.3* (pg.270, CRH).

→ Solve for original velocity at Point B:

$$(d_b)_{sand} = \frac{V_B^2 - V_C^2}{30(f \pm G)} \rightarrow 90ft = \frac{V_B^2 - (20mph)^2}{30(0.40)} \therefore V_B = 38.471mph$$

Note: *The variable for grade "G" is zero as no grade is present.*

→ Solve for original velocity at Point A (start of skid marks):

$$(d_b)_{asphalt} = \frac{V_A^2 - V_B^2}{30(f \pm G)} \rightarrow 120ft = \frac{V_A^2 - (38.471mph)^2}{30(0.75)} \therefore V_A = 64.653mph \quad \underline{\textbf{\textit{Answer: B}}}$$

---

20. After deducing that the roadway is a horizontal curve, use equations from *Section 5.2* (pg.271, CRH) to find the middle ordinate distance.

→ Set up equation for middle ordinate distance (M):

$$M = R - (R)\cos(\tfrac{\Delta}{2})$$

Find Radius of circular curve (R) and intersection angle (Δ, degrees):

$$\rightarrow R = \frac{5,729.6}{D} = \frac{5,729.6}{6.5} = 881.5ft$$

$$\rightarrow \Delta = 50°$$

$$\therefore M = 881.5ft - (881.5ft)\cos(\tfrac{50°}{2}) = \textbf{82.59ft} \quad \underline{\textbf{\textit{Answer: D}}}$$

---

21. Knowing that the curve is horizontal, equations from *Section 5.2* (pg.271, CRH) can be utilized to determine station of PT.

Note: The methods used for finding distances/stations along horizontal curves are different from vertical curves. To find station PT on a horizontal curve, one must remember that you have to begin at station PI then subtract the tangent length then add arc length. Simply adding tangent length to station PI will yield the wrong station for PT in most instances.

→ Set up equation to solve for station PT, starting at station PI:

$$STA_{PT} = STA_{PI} - T + L$$

Find tangent length (T) and arc length (L):

$$\rightarrow T = R\tan(\tfrac{\Delta}{2}) = (600ft)\tan(\tfrac{40°}{2}) = 218.382ft$$

$$\rightarrow L = \frac{R\Delta\pi}{180} = \frac{(500ft)(40°)\pi}{180} = 418.879ft$$

$$\therefore STA_{PT} = (15+00) - 218.382ft + 418.879ft = \textbf{17+00} \quad \underline{\textbf{\textit{Answer: C}}}$$

22.   With the provided diagram and context clues, it can be deduced that equations for vertical curve design (pg.278, CRH) must be used. From visual inspection of the diagram, it can be reasonably assumed that the portion of the bridge that is closest to the road will be the bottom right corner. Knowing this, the bridge elevation can be found by finding elevation on the point of the road directly under the corner.

→ Use curve elevation formula for station 4+75:

$$ELEV_{4+75}=Y_{PVC}+g_1x+x^2\left(\frac{g_2-g_1}{2L}\right)$$

Find variables:

$Y_{PVC}=740ft$

$g_1=-0.02$ *(keep grades in decimal format for vertical curves)*

$g_2=0.013$

$x=STA_{Bridge}\text{-}STA_{PVC}=475ft\text{-}321ft=154ft$

$L=STA_{PVT}\text{-}STA_{PVC}=520ft\text{-}321ft=199ft$

$\therefore ELEV_{4+75}=740ft+(-0.02)(154ft)+(154ft)^2\left(\frac{(0.013)-(-0.02)}{2(199ft)}\right)=738.886ft$

→ Find elevation of bridge:

$ELEV_{Bridge}=738.886ft+20ft\ clearance=\textbf{759ft}$ **Answer: A**

---

23.   To find station of the point with maximum elevation, the distance to the elevation turning point must be found. This can be found by using the equation for horizontal distance to max/min, x_m (pg.278, CRH).

→ Find distance to maximum:

$$x_m=\frac{g_1L}{g_1-g_2}=\frac{0.027(1,375ft-1,153ft)}{(0.027)-(-0.018)}=133.2ft$$

$\therefore STA_{max}=133ft+STA_{PVC}=133ft+1,153ft=\textbf{12+86}$ **Answer: A**

24.   The key word "USCS" is a prime indicator that the *Unified Soil Classification System* should be utilized for this problem (pg.116, CRH).

→ Follow classification steps in the *Soil Classification Chart*:

% passing No. 200 sieve=34 ∴ coarse-grained soil (sand and gravels)

% passing No. 4 sieve=46 ∴ gravel

Tip: *Be conscientious for the word changes between "retained" and "pass". These can easily become mixed up in meaning when in a rush.*

% passing No. 200 (fines) > 12% ∴ gravel with fines

Classification is now between GM and GC

→ Use liquid and plastic limits to plot point on the *Plasticity Chart* (pg.117, CRH):

Liquid Limit=25

Plasticity Index=Liquid Limit-Plastic Limit=12

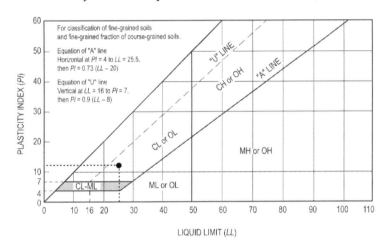

Soil plots in the "CL or OL" section ∴ group is **GC**   **Answer: D**

---

25.   Due to the implementation of hammer efficiency, the *Hammer Efficiency* equation should be used to make the proper adjustments (pg.130, CRH).

→ Adjust for hammer efficiency for each sample:

$$(N_{60})_1=\left(\frac{85\%}{60}\right)(32)=45.333$$

$$(N_{60})_2=\left(\frac{85\%}{60}\right)(35)=49.583$$

$$(N_{60})_3=\left(\frac{85\%}{60}\right)(30)=42.5$$

→ Find the average N-value:

$$(N_{60})_{Avg}=\frac{45.333+49.583+42.5}{3}=45.8$$

→ Use *Table 3-9* to relate N-value to relative density (pg.131, CRH):

$(N_{60})_{Avg}=45.8 \therefore$ ***Dense*** <u>***Answer: C***</u>

---

26. The formula for finding *Rock Quality Designation* can be found in *Section 3.7.4* (pg.126, CRH).

→ Set up the equation for RQD:

$$RQD=\frac{\Sigma Length\ of\ core\ pieces\ greater\ than\ 4in}{Total\ length\ of\ core\ (in)}=\frac{7in+5in+9in+6in+6in}{4ft(\frac{12in}{1ft})}=68.8\%$$

→ Use RQD to determine rock quality with *Figure 3-17* (pg.126, CRH):

$RQD=68.8\% \therefore$ ***Fair*** <u>***Answer: C***</u>

---

27. Given the soil's environmental conditions, it can be safely assumed that dry unit weight should be found. Use the relationship equations in *Section 3.8.3* to find dry unit weight (pg.139, CRH).

→ Set up formula for dry unit weight:

$$\gamma_d=\frac{G_s\gamma_w}{1+e}$$

Find void ration (e):

$$e=\frac{wG_s}{S}$$

$$w=\frac{W_W-W_D}{W_D}=\frac{53g-46g}{46g}=0.152=15.2\%$$

$$\therefore e=\frac{0.152(2.6)}{1}=0.396$$

Note: *Saturation is equal to 1 since the sample is described as saturated, otherwise, it must be found.*

$$\therefore \gamma_d=\frac{2.6(62.4\frac{lb}{ft^3})}{1+0.396}=116.2\frac{lb}{ft^3}$$ <u>***Answer: A***</u>

28. The equations for infinite slope failure in *Section 3.6.4* can be used to find factor of safety for failure with and without pore water pressure (pg.111, CRH).

***Tip:** Often, questions will include non-necessary information to lead you in the wrong direction. Carefully pick out only information that is required to obtain the answer.*

→ Set up factor of safety formula:

$$FS=\frac{\tan(\phi')}{\tan(\beta)}=\frac{\tan(37°)}{\tan(32°)}=1.2 \quad \textbf{\textit{Answer: A}}$$

---

29. The key word "overturn" means that the moments acting on the wall must be calculated about the toe (front) edge. Factor of safety for overturn is typically found by taking the ratio of moments preventing overturn to moments causing overturn.

→ Set up factor of safety equation:

$$FS_{Overturn}=\frac{\Sigma Moment\ Resisting}{\Sigma Moment\ Applying}$$

→ Find moments applying active overturn force (pg.78, CRH):

$$K_a=tan^2(45-\phi'2)=tan^2(45-30°2)=0.333$$

$$\therefore Active\ force=P_a=12K_a\gamma z^2=12(0.333)(120lbft3)(12ft-1ft)^2=2,417.58lb$$

$$\therefore Active\ moment=2,417.58lb(13x11ft)=8,864.46lb\text{-}ft$$

→ Find moments resisting overturn:

***Note:** Resisting moments will include the moments produced from the wall itself and soil on top of the heel edge (back side of the wall).*

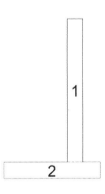

$$(W_{Concrete})_1=(6ftx1ft)(150lbft3)=900lb\ per\ linear\ foot\ of\ wall$$

$$(W_{Concrete})_2=(11ftx1ft)(150lbft3)=1,650lb\ per\ linear\ foot\ of\ wall$$

$$W_{Soil}=(10ftx1ft)(120lbft3)=1,200lb\ per\ linear\ foot\ of\ soil$$

$$\therefore$$

$$\Sigma Moment_{Resist}=(900lb)(3ft)+(900lb)(4.5ft)+(1,200lb)(5.5ft)=16,725lb\text{-}ft$$

→ Solve for FS:

$$FS_{Overturn}=16,725lb\text{-}ft8,864lb\text{-}ft=1.9 \quad \textbf{\textit{Answer: B}}$$

30. Earthquakes cause rapid vibrational forces within soils. Certain soil types are especially more susceptible to failure under vibration than others. For instance, when sand is subject to vibratory forces, it will become highly unstable, almost like quicksand. Sandier soils are especially susceptible to liquefaction if the soil is saturated.

→ Use group classification symbols to determine the sandiest soil:

MH=High plasticity silt

CL=Low plasticity clay

GW=well-graded gravel

SW=Well-graded sand   **Answer: D**

---

31. Settlement time is affected by many variables according to *Section 3.2.3* (pg.90, CRH). However, distance to drainage boundary (H_d) has the greatest affect on settlement time as it controls the denominator. This means that the foundation with the shortest distance to a drainage boundary will reach ultimate settlement sooner. Because **footer A** has both a drainage boundary of sand on top of the clay layer and a gravel layer underneath, it should reach ultimate settlement sooner.

Answer: B

---

32. In order to answer the question, the difference between disturbed and undisturbed sampling should be understood. Undisturbed soil samples will closely replicate the in-situ (original place) soil conditions as they were at the time and location of sampling whereas disturbed sampling does not.

Using this knowledge, it can be determined that both gradation and soil classification do not require in-situ conditions since these characteristics are only reliant on grain distributions.

Answer: A

---

33. Use effective stress formula for each substrata layer to find effective stress at A.

→ Set up effective stress formula to account for all layers:

$$\sigma'_A = (\gamma_{d,sand})(H_{dry\ sand}) + (\gamma_{wet,sand} - \gamma_w)(H_{wet\ sand}) + (\gamma_{wet,clay} - \gamma_w)(H_{clay})$$

Find wet unit weight for sand and clay:

$$\gamma_{wet,sand}=(\gamma_{d,sand})(1+w)=(130\tfrac{lb}{ft^3})(1+0.42)=184.6\tfrac{lb}{ft^3}$$

$$\gamma_{wet,clay}=(\gamma_{d,clay})(1+w)=(130\tfrac{lb}{ft^3})(1+0.36)=176.8\tfrac{lb}{ft^3}$$

$$\therefore \sigma_A'=(130\tfrac{lb}{ft^3})(2ft)+(184.6\tfrac{lb}{ft^3}-62.4\tfrac{lb}{ft^3})(7ft)+(176.8\tfrac{lb}{ft^3}-62.4\tfrac{lb}{ft^3})(6ft)=1,802\tfrac{lb}{ft^2}$$

Answer: D

---

34. Bearing capacity equations can be found in *Section 3.4.2* (pg.96, CRH). The footer in question is a simple strip footer which does not require usage of shape factors. However, depth of the footer must be accounted for which is not always the case in questions.

→ Set up equation for bearing capacity:

$$q_{ult}=c(N_c)+q(N_q)+0.5(\gamma_{soil})(B_f)(N_\gamma)$$

Use Bearing Capacity Factors table to find N_c, N_q, and N_γ (pg.97, CRH):

$\phi=43°\therefore N_c=105.1,\ N_q=99,\ N_\gamma=186.5$

$c=375psf$

$\gamma_{soil}=125\tfrac{lb}{ft^3}$

$q=Depth(\gamma_{soil})=2.5ft(125\tfrac{lb}{ft^3})=312.5\tfrac{lb}{ft^2}$

$B_f=4ft$

$$\therefore q_{ult}=(375psf)(105.1)+(312.5\tfrac{lb}{ft^2})(99)+0.5(125\tfrac{lb}{ft^3})(4ft)(186.5)=116,975\tfrac{lb}{ft^2}$$

→ Account for depth:

$$q_{ult}=116,975\tfrac{lb}{ft^2}-(Depth)(\gamma_{soil})=116,975\tfrac{lb}{ft^2}-(2.5ft)(125\tfrac{lb}{ft^3})=116,662.5\tfrac{lb}{ft^2}$$

→ Implement factor of safety:

$$FS=\frac{q_{ult}}{q_{all}}\rightarrow 2=\frac{116,662.5\tfrac{lb}{ft^2}}{q_{all}}\ \therefore q_{all}=58,331.25\tfrac{lb}{ft^2}x\frac{1k}{1000lb}=58\tfrac{k}{ft^2}\quad \underline{\textbf{\textit{Answer: C}}}$$

35. Equations for column strength can be found in *Section 1.6.8* (pg.36, CRH). Effective slenderness ratio is the main variable (*KL/r*) that dictates critical buckling stress since it is in the denominator.

Answer: C

---

36. Since beam deflection is to be found, *Section 1.6.7* should be used to set up a deflection equation based on loading conditions. Total deflection can be found by combining the results from both a point load formula and a distributed load formula (pg.35, CRH).

→ Set up equation for total deflection:

$$(v_{Max})_{Total}=(-\frac{Pa^2}{6EI})(3L-a)+(-\frac{wL^4}{8EI})$$

Find variables:

$P=10k=10,000lb$

$a=10.333ft=124in$

$E=29x10^6psi$

$L=10.333ft=124in$

$w=1\frac{k}{ft}x\frac{1000lb}{1k}x\frac{1ft}{12in}=83.333\frac{lb}{in}$

→ Find moment of inertia for hollow tube (pg.25, CRH):

$$I_{x,c}=\pi(a^4-b^4)/4=\pi[(3in)^4-(2.5in)^4]/4=32.938in^4$$

→ Solve for total deflection:

$$(v_{Max})_{Total}=[-\frac{(10,000lb)(124in)^2}{6(29x10^6psi)(32.938in^4)}(3(124in)-124in)]+[-\frac{(83.333lb/in)(124in)^4}{8(29x10^6psi)(32.938in^4)}]$$

$$=[-6.653in]+[-2.578in]=-9.231in \therefore 9.231in \quad \underline{\textit{Answer: A}}$$

37. In order to locate the point of maximum moment, a shear and moment diagram should be created to better visualize the forces acting within the beam.

$\rightarrow$ Find moment about the roller connection:

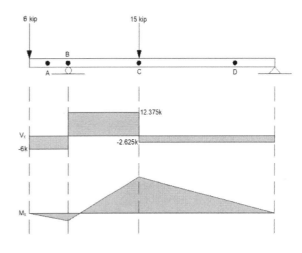

$\Sigma M_{Roller}=0=R_{Pin}(14ft)-15k(3.25ft)+6k(2ft)$

$\therefore R_{Pin}=2.625k$

$\Sigma F_y=0=R_{Roller}+2.625k-15k-6k$

$\therefore R_{Roller}=18.375k$

$\rightarrow$ Plot reactions on a shear diagram and use areas to plot a generalized moment diagram:

*Maximum occurs at **Point C***

Answer: C

---

38. When concrete fails due to shear, it is general knowledge that there is a typical angle of failure that often occurs. The typical angle of failure is known as the failure plane.

$\rightarrow$ *Failure plane of concrete*$=45+\frac{\phi}{2}=45+\frac{31°}{2}=$**61°** ***Answer: A***

---

39. In most cases, starting with a force balance equation is the best way to begin when asked to solve for concrete beam strength. A force balance equation can be derived from *Section 4.3.2.2* (pg.262, CRH).

$\rightarrow$ Set up force balance equation:

$(F)_{Concrete}=(F)_{Steel}\rightarrow 0.85f'_cab=A_sf_y$

$f'_c=4,000psi$

$b=12in$

$f_y=60ksi=60,000psi$

$A_s=2(\#9\ bar)=2(1in^2)=2in^2$

Tip: *Use rebar sizing table in Section 4.3.1 to acquire rebar information (pg.258, CRH).*

Solve for a:

$\rightarrow 0.85(4,000psi)a(12in)=(2in^2)(60,000psi)$ $\therefore a=2.94in$

Note: *Since a=2.94in, the compression area does not reach beyond the top flanges. Otherwise, the problem becomes slightly more complicated as A_c would be asymmetrical about the x-axis.*

→ Set up equation for nominal moment (pg.262, CRH):

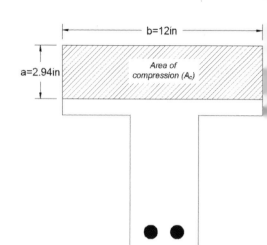

$$M_n = A_s f_y \left(d - \frac{a}{2}\right) = (2in^2)(60,000psi)\left(15in - \frac{2.94in}{2}\right)$$

$$\therefore M_n = 1,623,600in\text{-}lb \; x \; \frac{ft}{12in} \; x \; \frac{1k}{1,000lb} = \textbf{135k-ft}$$

Answer: B

---

40.   Poisson's ratio is defined as the ratio of lateral deformation to axial deformation as a result of strain.

Poisson's ratio can be expressed as: $v = \dfrac{\Delta\varepsilon_{lateral}}{\Delta\varepsilon_{axial}}$

Answer: D

7. Practice Exam II

1. A standard brick has dimensions as seen below. A single brick thick wall is to be constructed out of standard sized bricks with $\frac{1}{2}$in mortar fill between bricks. If the wall is 100ft long and 7ft tall, how many bricks are to be used and what is the total volume of mortar?

A. 4,325 and 0.8 CY
B. 4,500 and 1 CY
C. 4,511 and 1.8 CY
D. 4,675 and 2 CY

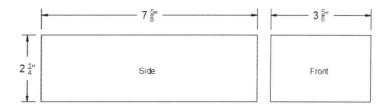

2. Find the critical path of the activity schedule below.

A. ABEHIK
B. ABDHIK
C. ACGJK
D. ABEIK

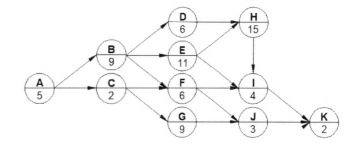

3. Excavation at a depth of 5ft must occur for the placement of a matt foundation. How many trucks of loose soil will have to be hauled off site if each truck can hold 5CY and the soil has an 8% expansion factor?

A. 280
B. 281
C. 285
D. 287

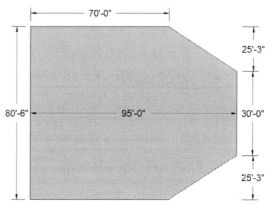

4. A surveyor has a total station set up over point A. If she has read a measurement of 3.538ft in the foresight, what is the elevation for point B?

A. 260.25 ft
B. 265.31 ft
C. 271.86 ft
D. 272.58 ft

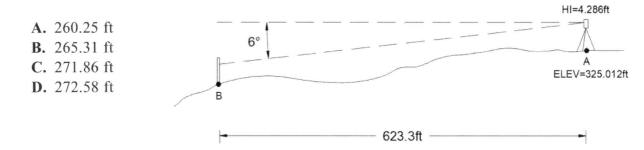

HI=4.286ft

6°

A
ELEV=325.012ft

B

623.3ft

5. According to the particle size distribution chart, soils A and B can be classified as:

A. Gap graded and well graded
B. Uniformly graded and gap graded
C. Uniformly graded and well graded
D. Gap graded and uniformly graded

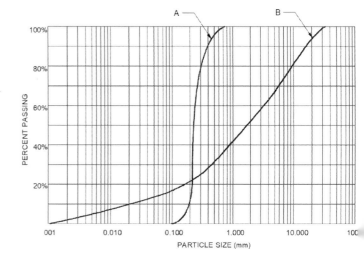

6. An all-terrain crane is used to place construction materials on the top floor of a building. If the carrier can come no closer than 30ft from the building face, how far away from the building edge can materials be placed if using maximum boom length and angle?

A. 18.6 ft
B. 19.2 ft
C. 20.1 ft
D. Does not clear building height

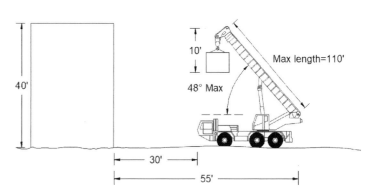

7.   What type of water is suitable for usage in structural concrete?

   A. Water with pH > 7
   B. Water that is free of suspended solids
   C. Water with a pH < 7
   D. Any form of potable water

8.   What is the expected peak discharge at point A during a 10-year rainfall event?

A. $2.1\frac{ft^3}{s}$

B. $2.5\frac{ft^3}{s}$

C. $2.7\frac{ft^3}{s}$

D. $3\frac{ft^3}{s}$

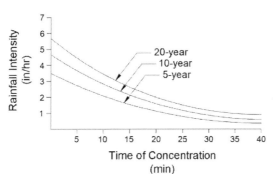 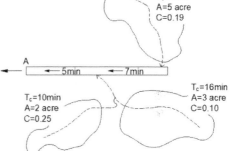

9.   What best describes supercritical flow?

   A. Fr < 1
   B. Fr > 1
   C. Fr = 1
   D. Not enough information

10.   A 1ft wide channel experiences a hydraulic jump. Find the Froude number after the hydraulic jump.

   A. 0.16
   B. 0.26
   C. 0.31
   D. 0.46

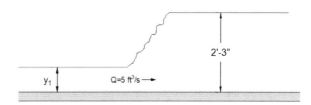

11. A levee is constructed to retain high water levels. Find the total discharge rate.

A. $0.092 \frac{ft^3}{min}$

B. $0.104 \frac{ft^3}{min}$

C. $0.121 \frac{ft^3}{min}$

D. $0.274 \frac{ft^3}{min}$

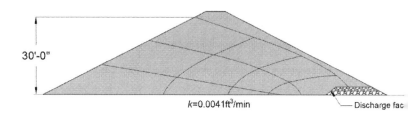

30'-0"

k=0.0041ft³/min

Discharge fac

12. Water flows through a diameter reducing pipe fitting. Find the approximate diameter required at point C if the velocity must be doubled from point B.

A. 2 in

B. 4.5 in

C. 5 in

D. 6 in

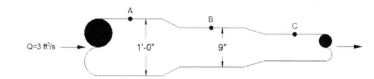

A

B

C

Q=3 ft³/s

1'-0"

9"

13. Four channels are proposed for a roadside ditch. Which channel will have the highest flow velocity?

A. Channel A

B. Channel B

C. Channel C

D. Channel D

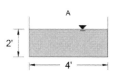

A

2'

4'

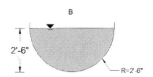

B

2'-6"

R=2'-6"

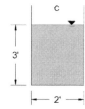

C

3'

2'

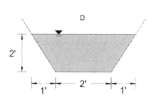

D

2'

1' 2' 1'

14. A rectangular open channel supports a flow rate of 320cfs at a downgrade slope of 0.2%. What is most nearly the most effective channel depth if $n=0.0012$?

 A. 1'-0"
 B. 1'-3"
 C. 1'-9"
 D. 2'-0"

15. An uphill pipe section experiences a total head loss due to friction of 2ft. The flow velocity is required to remain the same from point A to point B. What is the total head added by the pump?

 A. 103.2 ft
 B. 110.5 ft
 C. 114.7 ft
 D. 114.8 ft

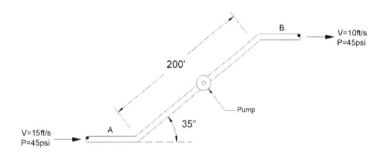

16. Underlying soil has been determined to have the following properties. What is the expected lateral pressure at point A?

 A. 1,352 psf
 B. 1,637 psf
 C. 1,703 psf
 D. 1,756 psf

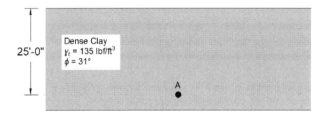

17. A new retaining wall is constructed to make way for roadway developments. Find the factor of safety against sliding. Unit weight of the concrete is 150 pcf.

A. 2.1
B. 4.7
C. 5.2
D. 5.6

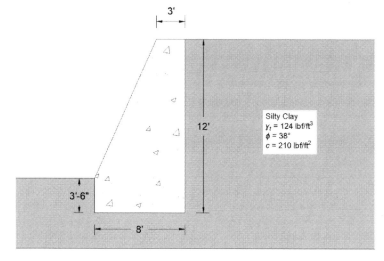

18. Find the active force resisted by the retaining wall. Friction between wall and soil is found to be 15°.

A. 3,398 psf
B. 3,937 psf
C. 5,003 psf
D. 5,173 psf

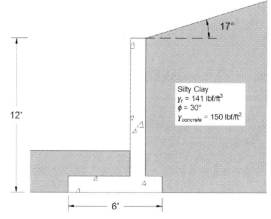

19. A construction site is to be dewatered from 4ft below grade to 14ft below grade in preparation for excavation. What is the change in effective stress at point A?

A. 537 psf
B. 587 psf
C. 602 psf
D. 624 psf

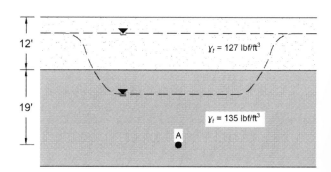

20. Which method of sediment control is often times used on construction sites?

    A. Dewatering bags
    B. Silt fencing
    C. Vegetative buffers
    D. All of the above

21. A 5ft wide footing is located between a right of way line and a retaining wall. What is the minimum footer length required if it is to support a 30 kip load. Ultimate bearing capacity of the underlying soil has been determined to be 2,000 psf.

    A. 2 ft
    B. 2.5 ft
    C. 3 ft
    D. Not enough information

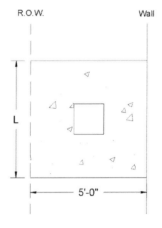

22. A square pedestal foundation supports a point load of 15 kips. Find the increase in stress 30 feet below the pedestal's edge.

    A. 29 psf
    B. 32 psf
    C. 66 psf
    D. 80 psf

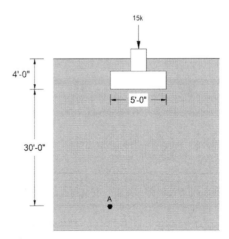

23. Heavy equipment is to be stored at a site bordering an existing retaining wall. How close to the wall's front face can equipment be placed if no extra pressure can be applied to any portion of the wall?

A. 23 ft
B. 25 ft
C. 26 ft
D. 27 ft

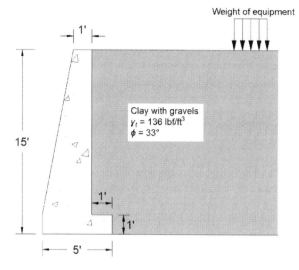

24. Surcharging is utilized for a normally consolidated clay soil. Determine the ultimate consolidated for the clay layer.

A. 6.6 in
B. 7 in
C. 7.4 in
D. 8 in

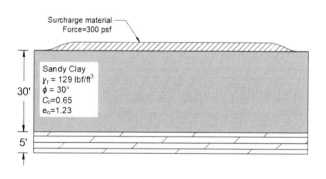

25. A sieve analysis was performed on a soil sample. Results are found below. Determine the AASHTO soil classification and Group Index number.

A. A-2-7; GI=2
B. A-2-4; GI=3
C. A-6; GI=7
D. A-4; GI=7

Seive No.	% Passing
No. 4	96
No. 40	84
No. 200	56

Liquid Limit	31
Plastic Limit	12

26. A soil sample has an initial weight of 42lb with a total volume of 0.35ft³. The sample is later oven dried and has a new weight of 35lb. Specific gravity is determined to be 2.48. What is the maximum moisture content that the soil can contain before experiencing swelling or bleeding?

A. 19.5%
B. 22.1%
C. 25.1%
D. 27.6%

27. A proposed roadway is required by local code to meet a minimum value of 2. With the following layer coefficients, find the required thickness for the aggregate base.

A. 4 in
B. 3 in
C. 2 in
D. 1 in

Hot Mix Asphalt	3in	0.44
Road Mix	1in	0.20
Aggregate Base	D_3	0.13
Engineered Fill	3in	0.10

28. An inverse radius curved roadway is constructed to weave through two city buildings. Both curves have a radius of 1,500ft. Deflection angle is given as 30°. Find the required distance separating both curve tangents.

A. 275 ft
B. 342 ft
C. 397 ft
D. 402 ft

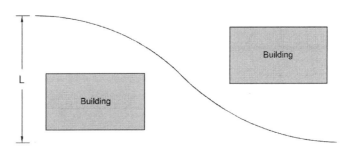

29. Two intersections are separated by a distance of 500ft. The redlights are designed to change signals sequentially with free flow traffic. If the traffic lights change signal at a 10 second difference in time, what is the design speed most nearly?

A. 20 mph
B. 25 mph
C. 30 mph
D. 35 mph

30. A contractor needs to know the station for the PI of a horizontal curve. Given station of PT and a curve radius of 3,240ft, find the station for PI.

A. 274+13
B. 295+96
C. 297+45
D. 301+23

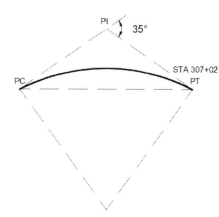

31. Find the tangent elevation at the yield sign location.

A. 614 ft
B. 630 ft
C. 633 ft
D. 641 ft

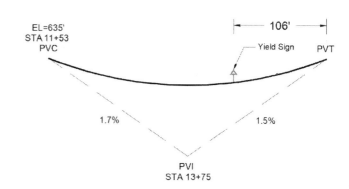

32. Edge of pavement for a new roadway is being staked out for compaction work. Distance from stake A and stake B has a bearing of N35°E and a length of 500ft. Distance from stake B to stake C has a bearing of S10°E and a length of 300ft. Find the departure and latitude required to close the loop from stake C.

    A. -330, -109
    B. -339, -114
    C. +339, +114
    D. +359. +109

33. A beam's ability to resist bending is mostly controlled by:

    A. Moment of inertia of cross-section
    B. Applied moments
    C. Beam stiffness
    D. Location of applied shear

34. A square HSS beam supports an overhead distributed load of 3k/ft. With a modulus of elasticity of 29×10^6 psi, find the expected deflection at the center of the beam.

    A. 2.5 in
    B. 3.0 in
    C. 3.4 in
    D. 3.8 in

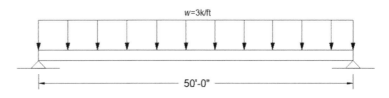

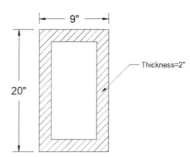

35.   A round HSS, 6" diameter, column has fixed connections at both ends. The column is 30ft in height with no bracing along its length. If the column is made from $\frac{1}{2}$in steel with $E=29\times10^6$ psi, find the maximum load allowed with a factor of safety of 1.5.

   A. 194 kips
   B. 201 kips
   C. 225 kips
   D. 232 kips

36.   Find if the following truss member is determinate and stable. If not, find the degree of indeterminacy.

   A. 1st degree indeterminacy and unstable
   B. 1st degree indeterminacy and stable
   C. Determinate and stable
   D. Determinate and unstable

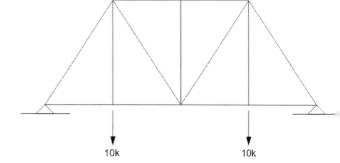

37.   A retaining wall is to be constructed with heavy rebar reinforcement. Determine the best layout for rebar.

   A. Section A
   B. Section B
   C. Section C
   D. Section D

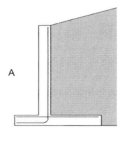
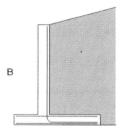
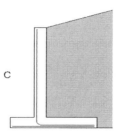
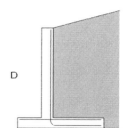

38. Determine the required area of steel for a concrete beam if the member must be able to resist a maximum moment reaction of 400k-ft. Concrete is subject to crush at $\varepsilon_c=0.003$; steel is subject to rupture at $\varepsilon_s=0.005$.

A. 0.209 in^2
B. 0.355 in^2
C. 0.401 in^2
D. 0.433 in^2

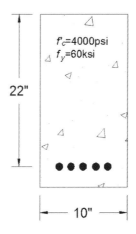

39. What is the most common reason for structural design to aim for steel yield before concrete rupture in regard to reinforced concrete beams in a building?

A. To transfer excess loading from concrete area to steel reinforcement.
B. To allow steel to reach plastic limit.
C. To give building occupants time to evacuate before complete failure.
D. To allow concrete to bear remaining tensile forces after steel failure.

40. Columns are erected to support the roof of a building. If designing load capacities for the winter months, snow load must be considered. Heavy snowfall generates an average load of 0.5ksf, wind load is 1ksf and dead load is 2ksf. Find the tributary load transferred to the middle column.

A. 1,300 kip
B. 1,400 kip
C. 1,500 kip
D. 1,600 kip

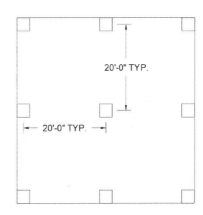

8. Practice Exam II Solutions

No.	Answer	No.	Answer
1	C	21	C
2	A	22	C
3	B	23	B
4	A	24	A
5	C	25	C
6	A	26	B
7	D	27	C
8	D	28	D
9	B	29	D
10	B	30	C
11	A	31	C
12	D	32	B
13	B	33	A
14	C	34	C
15	D	35	A
16	B	36	B
17	D	37	B
18	B	38	D
19	D	39	C
20	D	40	B

1. Using the area of a single brick and mortar, the required amount of bricks to construct the wall can be found by dividing the total area of wall by the single brick area.

Tip: Working with fractional inches can be tricky. Converting these to decimal inches before starting the problem can make the problem solving process less confusing and often times quicker.

→ Find total area of wall and single brick with mortar:

$$A_{wall}=LxH=100ftx7ft=700ft^2$$

$$A_{brick+mortar}=(L_{brick}+L_{mortar})(H_{brick}+H_{mortar})=(7.625in+0.5in)(2.25in+0.5in)$$

$$=22.344in^2 \rightarrow 22.344in^2 x\frac{1ft^2}{144in^2}=0.155ft^2 \text{ per brick}$$

→ Find total number of bricks to construct wall:

$$Quantity_{bricks}=A_{wall} \div A_{brick+mortar}=700ft^2 \div 0.155ft^2 = \textbf{4,511 bricks}$$

→ Find volume of wall and single brick without mortar:

$$V_{wall}=AxD=700ft^2x(3.625inx\frac{1ft}{12in})=211.458ft^3$$

$$V_{brick}=LxWxD=7.625inx2.25inx3.625in=62.191in^3$$

$$\rightarrow 62.191in^3 x\frac{1ft^3}{1728in^3}=0.036ft^3/brick$$

$$\therefore V_{mortar}=V_{wall}-4,511(V_{brick})=211.458ft^3-4,511(0.035ft^3)=49ft^3x\frac{1CY}{27ft^3}=\textbf{1.8 CY}$$

Answer: C

---

2. Finding critical path simply means to find the path with the longest duration. The critical path is defined as the series of activities that can not be delayed or the entire project duration will be affected. Use visual inspection to hypothesize at the longer activity paths.

→ Find which activity path yields the longest duration:

$$ACGJK=5+2+9+3+2=21$$

$$ACFIK=5+2+6+4+2=19$$

$$ABDHIK=5+9+6+15+4+2=41$$

$$ABEHIK=5+9+11+15+4+2=\textbf{46}$$

Answer: A

3. Finding the volume for abnormally shaped sites can sometimes be accomplished by breaking the sections up into multiple shapes for increased accuracy. For the provided construction site, the given area can be separated into square and trapezoid areas.

$\rightarrow$ Find volumes of square and trapezoid:

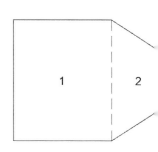

$$V_1 = LxWxD = 70ftx80.5ftx5ft = 28,175ft^3 x \frac{1CY}{27ft^3} = 1,043.519CY$$

$$V_2 = \frac{1}{2}(H)(L_1+L_2)(D) = \frac{1}{2}(95ft-70ft)(30ft+80.5ft)(5ft) = 6,906.25ft^3$$

$$\rightarrow 6,906.25ft^3 x \frac{1CY}{27ft^3} = 255.787CY$$

$\therefore$ Total volume = 1,043.519CY + 255.787CY = 1,299.306CY

$\rightarrow$ Use soil expansion formula to find loose volume from bank volume (pg.47, CRH):

$$V_L = (1+\frac{S_w}{100})V_B = (1+\frac{8\%}{100})(1,299.306CY) = 1,403.25CY$$

$\therefore$ Trucks = $V_{soil} \div V_{truck}$ = 1,403.25CY $\div$ 5CY = 280.65 trucks $\therefore$ **281 trucks**

Answer: B

---

4. Finding the elevation of a point from survey instrumentation is simply addition and subtraction of vertical distances. To find the elevation of point B, vertical distance from the instrument elevation to the point elevation must be found (pg.51, CRH)

$\rightarrow$ Find instrument elevation:

$Elev_{instrument} = Elev_A + Height\ of\ instrument = 325.012ft + 4.286ft = 329.298ft$

$\rightarrow$ Find vertical drop in elevation from instrument height to foresight reading:

$Elev_{foresight} = HI - tan(\theta)(Distance) = 329.298ft - tan(6°)(623.3ft) = 263.787ft$

$\rightarrow$ Find elevation of point B:

$Elev_B = Elev_{foresight} - Rod\ reading = 263.787ft - 3.538ft = $ **260.25ft** **Answer: A**

5. Grain size distributions generally fall within three different categories; well-graded, gap-graded and uniformly graded. *Section 2.1.5* of the reference handbook outlines the general shape of each category. Well-graded soils will have an even distribution of all grain sizes. Gap-graded soils are almost completely missing a certain range of particle sizes. Uniformly graded soils only contain a small range of particle sizes.

Answer: C

---

6. To find the building clearance the crane can reach will require proper use of trigonometry to identify both the vertical and horizontal capability of the crane. It is best to first determine if the crane is capable of vertical clearance, then solve for horizontal reach if clearance is satisfactory. Additional helpful information on cranes and crane components can be found in *Section 2.3* (pg.54, CRH).

$\rightarrow$ Find maximum vertical clearance of payload:

$Y_{payload}=Y_{boom}-Y_{payload\ drop}=sin(\theta)(L_{boom})-Y_{payload\ drop}=sin(48°)(110ft)-10ft=81.75ft$

$\rightarrow$ *81.75ft > 40ft ∴ vertical clearance is good*

$\rightarrow$ Find horizontal reach of boom:

$X_{boom}=cos(\theta)(110ft)=cos(48°)(110ft)=73.6ft$

∴ horizontal building clearance=73.6ft-55ft=18.6ft **Answer: A**

---

7. The concrete mixture process has various requirements that should be cleared in regard to the concrete application. One of the common requirements is the usage of water that is free of any minerals or chemicals that is detrimental to steel or the concrete itself. Although answer (B) proposes water that is free of suspended solids, the water must also be free of chemicals and option (B) does not specify this. However, option (D) is fully acceptable for concrete mixture as potable water is completely free of contaminants, suspended or diluted. Requirements for pH are typically not mentioned or monitored.

Answer: D

8. Given that the coefficients for runoff are given for each watershed is an easy indicator that flow rate can be found by utilizing the *Rational Formula Method* (pg.376, CRH). However, due to the inclusion of multiple watersheds, an average/compounded runoff coefficient must be found using the weighted average equation (pg.377, CRH).

→ Set up runoff flow rate equation:

$$Q_A = C_w I_{10\text{-}yr} A$$

→ Find input variables:

$$C_w = \frac{A_1 C_1 + A_2 C_2 + A_3 C_3}{A_1 + A_2 + A_3} = \frac{(2acre)(0.25) + (3acre)(0.10) + (5acre)(0.19)}{2acre + 3acre + 5acre} = 0.175$$

A=2acre+3acre+5acre=10acre

Time of concentration=longest path possible=16min+5min=21min

$I_{10\text{-}yr}$ *plots as approximately 1.75in/hr on chart*

→ Find flow rate:

$$Q_A = (0.175)(1.75in/hr)(10acre) = 3.063\frac{ft^3}{s} \quad \textbf{\textit{Answer: D}}$$

---

9. Critical state of flow is found with the Froude Number (pg.343, CRH). Without viewing *Section 6.4.3.1*, one could make the deduction that the prefix "super" would mean a Froude number greater than one.

Answer: B

---

10. Use *Section 6.4.8.1* to find the appropriate equations needed to obtain the Froude number after the jump. This can be accomplished by finding the initial depth of water before the jump then using initial depth to solve for the Froude number.

→ Set up equation to find Froude number:

$$\frac{y_1}{y_2} = \frac{1}{2}\left(\sqrt{1 + 8(Fr_2)^2} - 1\right)$$

→ Find y_1 by acquiring flow velocity after jump:

$$Q_2 = V_2 A_2 \rightarrow 5\frac{ft^3}{s} = V_2(2.25ftx1ft) \rightarrow V_2 = 2.222ft/s$$

$$\therefore y_1 = -\frac{1}{2}(y_2) + \sqrt{\frac{2v_2^2 y_2}{g} + \frac{y_2^2}{4}} = -\frac{1}{2}(2.25ft) + \sqrt{\frac{2\left(\frac{2.22ft}{s}\right)^2 (2.25ft)}{(32.2\frac{ft}{s^2})} + \frac{(2.25ft)^2}{4}} = 0.273ft$$

→ Find Froude number:

$$\frac{y_1}{y_2} = \frac{1}{2}(\sqrt{1 + 8(Fr_2)^2} - 1) \rightarrow \frac{0.273ft}{2.25ft} = \frac{1}{2}(\sqrt{1 + 8(Fr_2)^2} - 1) \therefore Fr_2 = 0.261 \quad \underline{\textit{Answer: B}}$$

---

11. Seepage through a levee can be measured as a volumetric flow rate based on the permeability of the fill material. *Section 3.14* outlines seepage and flow lines for multiple case scenarios (pg.188, CRH).

→ Set up flow rate equation:

$$Q = kh\left(\frac{N_f}{N_p}\right)$$

$$k = 0.0041\frac{ft}{min}$$

$$h = 30ft$$

N_f = Number of flow channels = 3

N_p = Number of potential drops (equipotential lines) = 4

$$\therefore Q = 0.0041\frac{ft}{min}(30ft)\left(\frac{3}{4}\right) = 0.092\frac{ft^3}{min} \textbf{ per unit width} \quad \underline{\textit{Answer: A}}$$

---

12. Flow rate is known to be conserved in closed conduit systems. Since flow rate is conserved, velocity at any point in the pipeline can be found by using the cross-sectional area.

→ Set up conservation of flow rate equation:

$$Q_A = Q_B = Q_C$$

Find flow rate at B:

$$Q_B = V_B A_B \rightarrow 3\frac{ft^3}{s} = V_B\left(\pi\left(\frac{0.75ft}{2}\right)^2\right) \rightarrow V_B = 6.79ft/s$$

→ Find required velocity and diameter for point C:

$$V_C = 2(V_B) = 2(6.79ft/s) = 13.581ft/s$$

$$\therefore 3\frac{ft^3}{s} = (13.581ft/s)A_C \rightarrow A_C = 0.221ft^2$$

$$A_C = 0.221ft^2 = \pi r^2 \therefore r = 0.265ft \rightarrow \textbf{D} = \textbf{0.53ft or 6in} \quad \underline{\textit{Answer: D}}$$

13. Finding flow velocity with only channel dimensions is not possible. However, relative flow velocity can be found by comparing the hydraulic radius of each channel. A higher hydraulic radius value correlates with higher flow velocity.

→ Find hydraulic radius of channel A:

$$R_A = \frac{A}{P} = \frac{(2ft)(4ft)}{2ft + 4ft + 2ft} = 1$$

→ Find hydraulic radius of channel B:

$$R_B = \frac{\frac{1}{2}(\pi(2.5ft)^2)}{\frac{1}{2}(2\pi(2.5ft))} = 1.25$$

→ Find hydraulic radius of channel C:

$$R_C = \frac{(2ft)(3ft)}{3ft + 2ft + 3ft} = 0.75$$

→ Find hydraulic radius of channel D:

$$R_D = \frac{\frac{1}{2}(2ft)(2ft + 4ft)}{2ft + 2(2.236ft)} = 0.92 \quad \text{*use Pythagorean theorem to find length of side walls}$$

Answer: B

---

14. The given variable "*n*" is usually an indicator that Manning's equation should be used (pg.345, CRH). Since dimensions of flow are not provided, the *Best Hydraulic Efficient Sections Without Freeboard* table can be used to find the most effective flow dimensions (pg.350).

→ Set up Manning's equation with table values substituted:

$$Q = (\frac{1.486}{n})(A)(R)^{\frac{2}{3}}\sqrt{s} \rightarrow Q = (\frac{1.486}{n})(2y^2)(\frac{1}{2}y)^{\frac{2}{3}}\sqrt{s}$$

→ Input given variables and isolate for *y*:

$$320cfs = (\frac{1.486}{0.0012})(2y^2)(\frac{1}{2}y)^{\frac{2}{3}}\sqrt{0.002} \therefore y = 1.77ft = 1'\text{-}9" \quad \underline{\textit{Answer: C}}$$

---

15. From a quick inspection, Bernoulli can be determined to be the best method for solving required pump head to be added. The energy line must be evaluated from point A to point B (pg.307).

→ Set up energy line equation (Bernoulli):

$$Z_A + \frac{P_A}{\gamma_w} + \frac{V_A^2}{2g} + h_{pump} = Z_B + \frac{P_B}{\gamma_w} + \frac{V_B^2}{2g} + h_f$$

→ Find elevation change:

$$H=\sin(\theta)(L)=\sin(35°)(220ft)=114.715ft$$

→ Input variables and isolate for h_{pump}:

$$0+\frac{45psi}{62.4\frac{lb}{ft^3}}+\frac{(\frac{15ft}{s})^2}{2(32.2\frac{ft}{s^2})}+h_{pump}=114.715ft+\frac{45psi}{62.4\frac{lb}{ft^3}}+\frac{(\frac{10ft}{s})^2}{2(32.2\frac{ft}{s^2})}+2ft$$

$$\therefore h_{pump}=114.8ft \text{ of added head} \quad \underline{\textit{Answer: D}}$$

---

16. Finding lateral pressure of a given point in soil substrata will require an at-rest coefficient. Similar to active and passive force coefficients, the at-rest coefficient can be found by using the soil internal friction value (pg.78, CRH).

→ Set up equation for lateral pressure at depth:

$$P_h=K_0 p_o$$

$$\rightarrow K_0=1-\sin(\phi)=1-\sin(31°)=0.485$$

$$\rightarrow p_0=D(\gamma_{soil})=(25ft)(135lbf/ft^3)=3,375lb/ft^2$$

$$\therefore P_h=(0.485)(3,375lb/ft^2)=1,637psf \quad \underline{\textit{Answer: B}}$$

---

17. Similar to factor of safety against overturning, the factor of safety against sliding is a ratio of the forces resisting sliding motion to forces driving slide. Forces that resist sliding include the weight of the wall causing friction against the underlying soil, cohesion of soil on the back face, and passive soil force. Driving forces primarily come from the soil active force (pg.80, CRH).

→ Set up equation for factor of safety:

$$FS_{slide}=\frac{F_{resist}}{F_{driving}}=\frac{W_w\tan(\phi)+P_p}{P_a}$$

→ Find variables:

$$W_w=(A_{trapazoid}+A_{square})(\gamma_{concrete})$$

$$=[((\tfrac{1}{2})(12ft-3.5ft)(8ft+3ft))+(3.5ftx8ft)](150lb/ft^3)=\underline{11,212.5lb/linear\ foot\ of\ wall}$$

$$P_p=\frac{1}{2}K_p(\gamma_{soil})(H)^2$$

$$\rightarrow K_p=\tan^2(45+\frac{\phi}{2})=\tan^2(45+\frac{38°}{2})=4.204$$

$$\therefore P_P = \frac{1}{2}(4.204)(124lbf/ft^3)(3.5ft)^2 = \underline{3,192.938lb/ft}$$

$$P_A = \frac{1}{2}(K_A)(\gamma_{soil})(H)^2$$

$$\rightarrow K_A = tan^2(45 - \frac{\phi}{2}) = tan^2(45 - \frac{38°}{2}) = 0.238$$

$$\therefore P_A = \frac{1}{2}(0.238)(124lbf/ft^3)(12ft)^2 = \underline{2,124.864}$$

$\rightarrow$ Find FS$_{slide}$:

$$FS_{slide} = \frac{(11,212.5lb)\,tan(38°) + 3,192.938lb/ft}{2,124.864lb/ft} = 5.625 \quad \textbf{\textit{Answer: D}}$$

---

18. Finding the active soil force imposed on a retaining wall from a sloped backfill is different than that of a level backfill. The inclined backfill will require usage of the Coulomb equation (pg.80, CRH).

$\rightarrow$ Set up equation for active force:

$$P_A = \frac{1}{2}(K_{A,Coulomb})(\gamma_{soil})(H)^2$$

$\rightarrow$ Find active force coefficient for a sloped backfill:

$$K_{A,Coulomb} = \frac{cos^2(\phi - \theta)}{cos^2(\theta)\,cos(\theta + \delta)[1 + \sqrt{\frac{sin(\phi + \delta)\,sin(\phi - \beta)}{cos(\theta + \delta)\,cos(\theta - \beta)}}]^2}$$

Tip: *The Coulomb equation for active force coefficient can be very lengthy for a scientific calculator. Try solving for the numerator and denominator separately, to avoid mistakes when typing in values, then divide the resultants.*

$\rightarrow$ *Find input angles:*

$\theta = 0°$

$\phi = 30°$

$\delta = 15°$

$\beta = 17°$

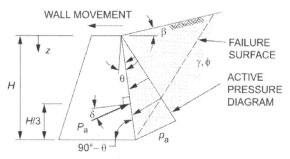

$\rightarrow$ Solve for active force coefficient:

$$K_{A,Coulomb} = \frac{cos^2(30 - 0)}{cos^2(0)\,cos(0 + 15)[1 + \sqrt{\frac{sin(30+15)\,sin(30-17)}{cos(0+15)\,cos(0-17)}}]^2} = \frac{0.75}{1.934} = 0.388$$

$$\therefore P_A = \frac{1}{2}(0.388)(141lbf/ft^3)(12ft)^2 = 3,937.085lb/ft \quad \textbf{\textit{Answer: B}}$$

19. The change in effective stress at point A will be based on the changing water level.

→ Find effective stress for both water levels:

$$\sigma'_{initial}=\Sigma(\gamma_{soil}-\gamma_w)(H)=(127\tfrac{lb}{ft^3})(4ft)+(\ 127\tfrac{lb}{ft^3}-62.4\tfrac{lb}{ft^3})(8ft)+(135\tfrac{lb}{ft^3}-62.4\tfrac{lb}{ft^3})(19ft)$$

$$=2,404.2psf$$

$$\sigma'_{final}=(127\tfrac{lb}{ft^3})(12ft)+(135\tfrac{lb}{ft^3})(2ft)+(135\tfrac{lb}{ft^3}-62.4\tfrac{lb}{ft^3})(17ft)=3,028.2psf$$

$$\therefore \Delta_{pressure}=3,028.2psf-2,404.2psf=\textbf{624psf} \quad \underline{\textbf{\textit{Answer: D}}}$$

---

20. Sediment control on a construction site serves the purpose of preventing pollutants and suspended solids from contaminating nearby water sources. This is typically achieved through the usage of silt fencing, dewatering bags and vegetative buffers. Each method will filter suspended solids from water that is passing through them.

Answer: D

---

21. The ultimate bearing capacity of a footer is a direct ratio of applied load to footer area which results in a pressure value.

→ Equate ultimate bearing (pressure) with load to area ratio:

Tip: A good indicator on how to solve problems such as this is units. Ultimate bearing capacity is given as a pressure ($\tfrac{lb}{ft^2}$) which means that a unit weight is divided by an area.

$$Q_{ult}=\frac{F}{A} \rightarrow 2,000\frac{lb}{ft^2}=\frac{30kip \ x \ \frac{1000lb}{1k}}{5ft \ x \ L} \quad \therefore L=3ft \quad \underline{\textbf{\textit{Answer: C}}}$$

---

22. Stress induced on soil by a footer will affect underlying soil based on distance from the footer. *Section 3.5.1* contains a stress distribution chart that can be used to approximate such affects (pg.100, CRH).

→ Find overall stress:

$$\sigma=\frac{F}{A}=\frac{15kip(\frac{1000lb}{1k})}{5ft \ x \ 5ft}=600psf$$

→ Find approximate depth factor by plotting point A on graph:

Depth factor is approximately 0.11 $\therefore \sigma_A=0.11(600psf)=\textbf{66psf}$ *Answer:C*

23. If additional load can not be affecting any portion of the retaining wall, then the failure plane for weight of equipment must be evaluated. The failure plane of the soil resulting from the additional weight of equipment must not touch the wall or heel of the wall.

→ Determine horizontal reach of failure plane:

$$\theta_{failure}=45+\frac{\phi}{2}=45+\frac{33°}{2}=61.5°$$

Distance from rightmost area of heel:

$$D_{heel}=\frac{15ft}{\tan(33°)}=23.098ft\ from\ heel$$

Distance from front face:

$$D_{front}=23.098ft+1ft+1ft=\textbf{25.098ft}\quad\underline{\textbf{\textit{Answer: B}}}$$

---

24. Surcharging is a common compaction practice for cohesive soils. A large amount of fill is placed on a surface and the weight of the fill causes compaction over time. Total compaction can be calculated if the change in pressure is known (pg.89, CRH).

→ Set up consolidation formula for a normally consolidated soil:

$$S_C=\Sigma_1^n\frac{C_c}{1+e_0}H_o\log_{10}(\frac{p_f}{p_o})$$

Find initial overburden stress (p_o) and final overburden stress (p_f):

→ $p_o=(H_{mid-layer})(\gamma_{soil})=(15ft)(129lbf/ft^3)=1,935lb/ft^2$

→ $p_f=p_o+\Delta p=1,935lb/ft^2+300lb/ft^2=2,235lb/ft^2$

∴ $S_C=(\frac{0.65}{1+1.23})(30ft)(\frac{2,235psf}{1,935psf})=0.547ft\ x\ \frac{12in}{1ft}=\textbf{6.568in}\quad\underline{\textbf{\textit{Answer: A}}}$

---

25. Soil classification can be achieved through multiple standards. This problem specifies that the AASHTO standard must be used to classify the given soil (pg.124, CRH).

→ Use % passing to find group classification:

% passing No.200 sieve=56% ∴ silty-clay material

% passing No.200 sieve=56% ∴ A-4 or A-6 category

→ Use Atterberg limits to further classify soil:

Liquid limit=31 ∴ A-4 or A-6

Plasticity index=liquid limit-plastic limit=31-12=19 ∴ A-6

$\rightarrow$ Find Group Index to verify result:

$$GI=(F\text{-}35)[0.2+0.005(LL\text{-}40)]+0.01(F\text{-}15)(PI\text{-}10)$$

$$=(56\text{-}35)[0.2+0.005(31\text{-}40)]+0.01(56\text{-}15)(19\text{-}10)=6.945 \rightarrow 7$$

$\rightarrow$ *GI=7<16* ∴ *A-6*   ***Answer: C***

---

26.   Soils will swell or "bleed" (expell water) when saturation reaches 100%. Using weight-volume formulas from tables provided in *Section 3.8.3*, the known saturation of 100% can be used to solve for moisture content (pg.139, CRH).

$\rightarrow$ Set up equation for saturation:

$$S=\frac{w(G)}{e}$$

$\rightarrow$ Use formula for dry unit weight to obtain void ratio:

$$\gamma_d=\frac{W_d}{V}=\frac{35lb}{0.35ft^3}=100lb/ft^3$$

$$\gamma_d=\frac{G\gamma_w}{1+e} \rightarrow 100lb/ft^3=\frac{(2.48)(62.4\frac{lb}{ft^3})}{1+e} \therefore e=0.548$$

$\rightarrow$ Use formula for moisture content:

$$w=\frac{Se}{G}=\frac{(1)(0.548)}{2.48}=0.221 \therefore 22.1\% \quad \textit{\textbf{Answer:B}}$$

---

27.   Although not located in the *Civil Refernce Handbook*, the formula for roadway structural number is a common formula that many civil engineers are expected to know by memory.

$\rightarrow$ Set up structural number equation:

$$SN=\Sigma(a_n)(D_n)$$

$\rightarrow$ *2=0.44(3in)+(0.2(1in)+0.13(D_3)+0.1(3in)* $\rightarrow$ *D₃=1.385in*

∴ *Aggregate base must be roughly **2in or greater***   ***Answer: C***

28. Distance seperating both curve tangents can be found by calculating the middle ordinate distance for each respective curve. A summarized formula for this complete distance can be found in the reverse horizontal curves section (pg.276, CRH).

→ Set up equation for distance L:

$$p=(R_1+R_2)(1-cos(\Delta))=(1,500ft+1,500ft)(1-cos(30°))=\textbf{401.924ft} \quad \underline{\textbf{\textit{Answer: D}}}$$

---

29. Traffic lights that are in series are commonly designed so that cars that pass the first light on yellow can cruise through all lights on yellow meaning that subsequent lights are delayed by a few seconds from the first. Knowing this information, the delay time between the two traffic lights in the problem can be used to approximate design speed.

→ Set up velocity formula:

$$V=\frac{D}{t}$$

Distance traveled=500ft

Time to travel 500ft=10sec

$$\therefore V=\frac{500ft}{10sec}=50\frac{ft}{s} \rightarrow 50\frac{ft}{s}x\frac{60sec}{1min}x\frac{60min}{1hr}x\frac{1mile}{5280ft}=\textbf{34.091mph} \quad \underline{\textbf{\textit{Answer:D}}}$$

---

30. Use respective equations in *Section 5.2* to determine tangent and arc length (pg.273, CRH).

→ Set up equations to solve for tangent and arc lengths:

$$L=\frac{R\Delta\pi}{180}=\frac{(3,240ft)(35°)(\pi)}{180}=1,978.2ft$$

$$T=Rtan(\frac{\Delta}{2})=(3,240ft)tan(\frac{35°}{2})=1,021.568ft$$

→ Solve for station at PI:

$$STA_{PI}=STA_{PT}-L+T=30,702ft-1,978.2ft+1,021.568ft=\textbf{297+45} \quad \underline{\textbf{\textit{Answer: C}}}$$

31. Tangent and curve elevation are solved in similar methods. The only difference being the accounting for the parabola constant in curve elevation. *Section 5.3.1* provides a straightforward equation for finding tangent elevation at a given point (pg.278, CRH). Tangent elevation can also be solved by using basic slope computations.

→ Find horizontal distance from PVI to sign (x):

$$L_{curve}=(STA_{PSI}-STA_{PVC})(2)=(1,375ft-1,153ft)(2)=444ft$$

$$x=\frac{L}{2}-106ft=\frac{444ft}{2}-106ft=116ft$$

→ Use general slope computation for PVI and sign elevation:

$$Elev_{PVI}=Elev_{PVC}-g_1(\frac{L}{2})=635ft-(0.017)(\frac{444ft}{2})=631.226ft$$

$$Elev_{sign}=Elev_{PVI}+g_2(x)=631.226ft+(0.015)(116ft)=\textbf{632.966ft} \quad \underline{\textbf{\textit{Answer: C}}}$$

---

32. A bearing angle is defined as the angle in relation to the meridian divided into quadrants based on the cardinal directions. The departure and latitude of angles is summarized in *Section 5.2.5* (pg.276, CRH).

Tip: *It can be helpful to sketch and connect angles to obtain a better visual of the problem at hand.*

→ Sketch angles to form partial survey traverse:

→ Calculate total departure and latitude from A to C:

$$(Dep)_{AC}=sin(\theta)(L)=sin(35°)(500ft)=+286.788ft$$

$$(Lat)_{AC}=cos(\theta)(L)=cos(35°)(500ft)=+409.576ft$$

$$(Dep)_{BC}=sin(\theta)(L)=sin(10°)(300ft)=+52.094ft$$

$$(Lat)_{BC}=cos(\theta)(L)=cos(10°)(300ft)=-295.442ft$$

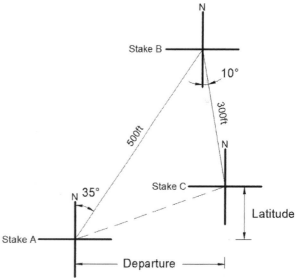

→ Calculate sum of departure and latitude:

$$\Sigma Dep=+286.788ft+52.094ft=338.882ft$$

$$\Sigma Lat=+409.576ft-295.442ft=114.134ft$$

$$\therefore (Dep)_{CA}=\textbf{-338.882ft}$$

$$\therefore (Lat)_{CA}=\textbf{-114.134ft} \quad \underline{\textbf{\textit{Answer: B}}}$$

33. Stress in a beam due to bending is variable with moment applied and the moment of inertia. The equation for normal stress within a beam is detailed in *Section 1.6.7.2* (pg.31, CRH). Moment of inertia of the cross section is the controlling variable as the denominator.

Answer: A

---

34. Beam deflection due to load can be calculated based on the loading scenario. For the loading scenario given, the equation for a double supported beam with distributed loading should be used (pg.34, CRH).

→ Set up equation for deflection:

$$y_{max} = -\frac{5wL^4}{384EI}$$

$$\rightarrow w = 3\frac{k}{ft} \times \frac{1ft}{12in} \times \frac{1000lb}{1k} = 250\frac{lb}{in}$$

$$\rightarrow L = 50ftx\frac{12in}{1ft} = 600in$$

$$\rightarrow E = 29x10^6 psi$$

Use moment of inertia table for I (pg.24, CRH):

$$\rightarrow I = [\frac{b_1 h_1^3}{12}] - [\frac{b_2 h_2^3}{12}] = [\frac{(9in)(20)^3}{12}] - [\frac{(9in-4in)(20in-4in)^3}{12}] = 4,293.333in^4$$

$$\therefore y_{max} = -\frac{5(\frac{250lb}{in})(600in)^4}{384(29x10^6 psi)(4,293.333in^4)} = -3.388in \rightarrow \textbf{3.4in total deflection}\quad \underline{\textit{\textbf{Answer: C}}}$$

---

35. Columns that have long, unbraced, sections are subject to a type of failure known as buckling. The critical load for column buckling can be calculated with Euler's Formula, as described in *Section 1.6.8* (pg.36, CRH).

→ Find variables required for Euler's Formula:

$$P_{cr} = \frac{\pi^2 EI}{(Kl)^2}\quad \textit{(Euler's)}$$

$$\rightarrow K = 0.5 \textit{ (fixed-fixed connection)}$$

$$\rightarrow l = 30ftx\frac{12in}{1ft} = 360in \textit{ (unbraced length)}$$

$$\rightarrow E = 29x10^6 psi$$

Use moment of inertia table for I (pg.24, CRH):

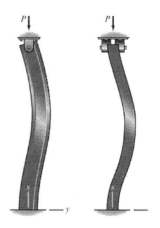

$$\rightarrow I = \frac{\pi(a^4 - b^4)}{4} = \frac{\pi((3in)^4 - (2.5in)^4)}{4} = 32.938in^4$$

$$\therefore P_{cr} = \frac{\pi^2(29x10^6 psi)(32.938in^4)}{((0.5)(360in))^2} = 290,971.169lb \ x \ \frac{1kip}{1000lb} = 291 \ kip$$

→ Apply factor of safety:

$$FS = \frac{P_{cr}}{P_{all}} \rightarrow 1.5 = \frac{291kip}{P_{all}} \ \therefore P_{all} = 194k \quad \underline{\textbf{\textit{Answer: A}}}$$

---

36. Determinacy and stability for a structure can be calculated using the total number of joints, members and reactions. Although not outlined in the reference manual, the equation to find determinacy and stability should be memorized by default.

→ Set up equations for determinacy and stability:

Determinacy=r+m-2j

Stable if (m+r) > 2j

  → *r=total number of reactions acting on truss*

  → *m=total number of members*

  → *j=total number of joints*

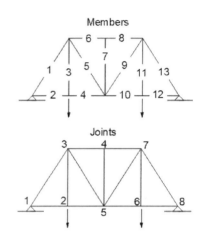

Members

Joints

→ Find determinacy:

Determinacy=4+13-2(8)=1

  → *Indeterminate if (r+m-2j) > 0*

  → *Degree of indeterminacy = number above 0*

 ∴ *indeterminate by 1ˢᵗ degree*

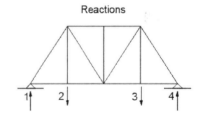

Reactions

→ Find stability:

Stability=m+r=13+4=17

17>2j=16

  → *Unstable if m+r<2j*

∴ *stable*

Answer: B

37.	Reinforcement, rebar, is added to concrete structures as a means to handle tensile forces. Concrete, although very resilient to compressive forces, does not hold a high tensile strength. Therefore, rebar is added to compensate for lack in tensile strength. If rebar were to be added to the retaining wall depicted, it would be best suited in areas experiencing tensile stress.

Tip: Creating a quick sketch of conceptual questions such as this can help better visualize forces acting on the wall and where tensile stress would occur.

→ Sketch general outline of forces acting on wall:

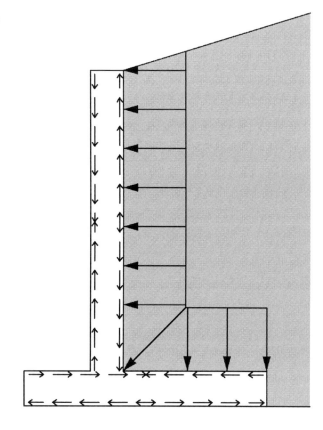

*→ As seen in the sketch, tensile forces are experienced in both the back face of the wall and the bottom. The only option presented that depicts rebar in all areas experiencing tensile stress is **B**.*

Answer: B

38. If tasked with finding capacity of a concrete beam with variables missing, it can commonly be assumed that the best course of action is to consult a stress-strain diagram for the respective member. The components to construct a stress-strain diagram are outlined in *Section 4.3.2.2* (pg.262, CRH).

→ Construct a stress-strain diagram for the cross section:

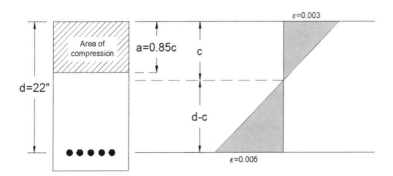

→ Set up equation for nominal moment capacity:

$$M_n = A_s f_y (d - \frac{a}{2})$$

→ Find *a* using diagram by equating tensile to compressive force:

$$\frac{0.003}{c} = \frac{0.005}{d-c} \rightarrow c = 0.375d \therefore c = 0.375(22in) = 8.25in$$

$$\rightarrow a = 0.85c \therefore a = 0.85(8.25in) = 7.013in$$

→ Solve for A_s in nominal moment equation:

$$M_n = 400k\text{-}ftx\frac{12in}{1ft}x\frac{1000lb}{1k} = 480,000lb\text{-}in$$

$$f_y = 60\frac{k}{in^2}x\frac{1000lb}{1k} = 60,000psi$$

$$\therefore 480,000lb\text{-}in = (A_s)(60,000psi)(22in\text{-}\frac{7.013in}{2}) \rightarrow \boldsymbol{A_s = 0.433in^2} \quad \underline{\textbf{\textit{Answer: D}}}$$

---

39. Steel reinforcement within concrete beams is almost always designed to fail before the concrete itself. When steel yields initially, it is easy to detect when a member is actively failing due to concrete chipping and cracking around the steel that is yielding. Since concrete failure usually occurs instantly, it is undesirable to design for it to occur before tensile failure.

Answer: C

40. Tributary area of a supporting column relies on the column's separation distance from other load bearing members. Total tributary load can be found by summing all loads acting within the respective member's tributary area.

Note: The phrase "TYP" is often used in civil designs to call out a typical detail that is true for all other similar occurrences (i.e. all of the columns in the given problem are 20ft apart as the label calls out "20ft TYP").

→ Find column tributary area:

$$A_{trib}=LxH=20ftx20ft=400ft^2$$

→ Calculate overbearing load:

$$F_{total}=0.5ksf+1ksf+2ksf=3.5ksf$$

→ Calculate total load transferred to column:

$$F_{column}=3.5\frac{k}{ft^2}x400ft^2=1,400k$$

Answer: B

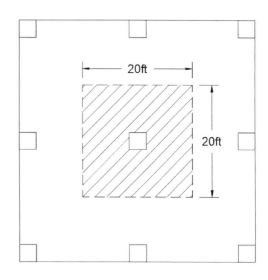

If you made it this far in the practice booklet, congratulations! You are now one step closer to passing the Civil PE. Thank you for picking up this book and as always, good luck!

Please do not hesitate to reach out regarding mistakes and calculation errors that may have been missed upon reviewal: **ethan.mccutcheon0@gmail.com**

Made in the USA
Las Vegas, NV
12 August 2023

75985865R00039